Married **Players** and the Women **that** worship them

A Woman's Guide to Escaping the Player Prison

J. G. David

Published by

J. G. David

ISBN: 978-0-615-48351-1

Printed in the United States

Library of Congress Cataloging-in-Publication Data

J. G. David

Married Players and the Women That Worship Them/ J. G. David

ISBN 978-0-615-48351-1

This publication is designed to provide information with regard to the subject matter covered. It is sold with the understanding that the author is not engaged in rendering legal, accounting, or other professional advice. If legal advice or other expert assistance is required, the services of competent professional person should be sought.

-From a *Declaration of Principles* jointly adopted by a committee of American Bar association and a Committee of Publishers and Associations.

This book is available at quantity discounts for bulk purchases. Please access *www.marriedplayersjd.com* for more information.

For my mother, Elaine. May the next life be kind to her.

With special thanks to Michael Dougher, Margaret Goldman, and David Dunaway for changing the direction of my life years ago.

Keep your thoughts positive, because your thoughts become your words. Keep your words positive, because your words become your behaviors. Keep your behaviors positive, because your behaviors become your habits. Keep your habits positive, because your habits become your values. Keep your values positive, because your values become your destiny.

-Ghandi

This book is for all those who hurt, even the Player.

Contents

Introduction

Introduction

Everyone knows the Cinderella story where the handsome prince rescues poor Cinderella from her horrible life and then whisks her away (on his horse) to live happily ever after. There the story ended. No one ever defined *happily ever after*. This is the unrealistic fantasy we learned when we were kids, where the Prince in shining armor gallops into our lives and saves us from distress. The sad reality is that many women spend the rest of their lives seeking the unrealistic fairytale with Mr. Prince when *happily every after* never arrives.

We will never know what *happily ever after* was for Cinderella. Some may wager that she would have jumped on the Prince's horse in order to avoid her evil stepmother's prison. No matter how bad the Prince turned out to be, Cinderella may have closed her eyes to any "red flags" or character flaws because he rescued her from hell. All she was able to see was the phony, charming image he presented.

Many women live this dysfunctional cycle all the time. *Married Players and Women That Worship Them* addresses this cycle of destruction and helps women explore options for making healthier decisions. This book is a resource that helps women transform their lives through self-reflection and serves as a tool for making the changes necessary for healthy transformation. Most importantly, it is a conduit of information that helps us understand the profile of the player and that of the women that worship them.

This book is a must read because, like Cinderella, many women are only able to see the fairytale image of the Prince. *Married Players and the Women That Worship Them* is designed to help women escape from the *Cinderella Syndrome*, as I call it. This book will help women break the cycle of torment, destruction, and devastation in their lives. Whether or not you are a mistress who has gotten entangled with a married man, or you are a scorned wife who has "lost" due to another woman somewhere, you will gain much insight and empowerment from the contents of this book. If you are reading this book now, then you or someone you know is *not* living happily ever after with a husband that belongs to another, or you are a wife who is *not* living happily after with a husband you thought would be faithful forever.

Betrayal is a silent, unrelenting world of emotional terror that many women will not discuss because they are ashamed. People do not want to hear them whine and complain about their relationships with married lovers. In turn, they fear being frowned upon and losing credibility. People also don't want to hear a wife complain again (for the hundredth time) about her suspicion that her husband is running around on her. The last thing she wants the world to know is that her husband "may not love her." This may be a direct reflection on the "terrible" wife she is (as the subconscious tape in her mind dictates), and it is this very reason that he sought comfort elsewhere.

We are happiest when we are loved, accepted and joined with another. Love makes us come alive, but when we are alone, isolated or betrayed, we feel just the opposite. It hurts like hell. Over time our self worth diminishes as the feeling of unworthiness ruins our lives. We then become emotionally unstable and find ourselves on a fast moving (emotional) roller coaster ride until, eventually, the coaster crashes and burns. The goal of this book is to help you get off the ride before it derails.

Whether or not you are a wife, suspicious of another woman, or a mistress, suspicious of the relationship he really has with his wife, it is absolute hell when you are not the only woman, especially when you know he is blatantly lying to you. A woman in this situation can literally go crazy because this type of man is a great con artist and manipulator. *Married Players and the Women That Worship Them* helps a woman identify the discrepancies between what he says and what he does. When he becomes emotionally schizophrenic, for example, the woman should dig deeper to find out what is really going on. If her instincts are screaming at her core that something is not right, then she needs to pay attention to her instincts. If she waits for him to tell her that she is crazy for being suspicious, then she will eventually become crazy.

You do not want to be a "fool" by giving your all to him while he is giving it to some other woman. The great atrocity of this scenario is that these men can be such great liars that it could be years before the woman puts all the pieces together. This book is designed to help you trust your instincts so that you may get the truth now. Why wait ten years to find the truth while your pretty years are passing you by? Now is the time to find happiness, with or without him.

I Just Know He Has Another Woman

If you have ever experienced a situation where something does not feel right with your man, you know it is a painful ordeal, especially if you are very much in love with him. You can feel the presence of something or someone "stealing" him away from you. You begin to feel alone, like you don't even have a friend anymore. He has one excuse after another (for his absences and avoidance behaviors) that you can't refute. If you do, you become the nagging "bitch" who is creating problems for no reason. Your mind begins to scratch and claw (metaphorically speaking) for the truth but, the more you dig, the less you find. Should you attempt to address your concern, he becomes defensive and hostile, cleverly shutting down the discussion. There is no where to turn. You feel heavy with uncertainty and insecurity. As you try to shrug off your gut instincts, you are left only with sleepless nights and bitchy days. You do not notice the beautiful spring days or the flowers that recently bloomed. You have nothing to look forward to anymore and find yourself in such a state of turmoil that you would eventually do anything to feel loved again. If you just knew for sure that he was faithful to you and that your mind was just playing tricks on you, you would be happy. You grieve for those days when he was your best friend, the days when he showered you with attention. It was then that he pursued you with fascination and interest that you came alive for the first time. Now he has forced you into the role of pursuer and you are miserable.

Once we are deceived, it is impossible to find peace. We can become bitter and "damaged" to future relationships. It is a desperate feeling of aloneness. This book will let women know they are not alone and will also expose the hurtful games these men play. I used numerous examples and testimonials, some real and some fictitious, to exemplify the points in this book. I share them with you in the hope that you will learn from them.

Please know that the contents in this book are not about condemnation or judgment. No matter what our religious or moral beliefs, it is imperative that we put aside our personal bias and understand the imminent dangers that may result from infidelity. Whether we think it is right or wrong to become involved with another woman's husband, for instance, does not matter as much as helping this woman make better choices for herself. Sometimes people are trapped and do not know how to exit a bad situation. The purpose of this book is to provide information so that she will move forward and can now make better choices for herself.

May the Other Woman Rise

There are many reasons women get caught in tangled webs with unfaithful men- many of them are players and some are just plain unfaithful wimps. We will define these types of men and explore reasons for their actions. It is so important that women understand these men and why they behave so poorly.

Many women are living in situations of torment for years that may have horrifying endings. The movie *Fatal Attraction*, for instance, is a prime example of what can culminate over time from being sucked into a married player's world of betrayal. Look at teenager Amy Fisher who shot the wife (of her married lover), Mary Jo Buttafuoco, in the face with a gun. Some women get entangled in webs with married men and do the unthinkable. They impulsively act out of momentary insanity because they just can't take anymore of the lies or the suspicious events that take place before their eyes.

Many women are still seeking the fairytale of the Prince in the castle, where the players rescue them from misery and fill the void(s) within them. If you know a woman in this situation, you know it is difficult to sit back and watch her waste her life for a "jerk." There is the tendency for her to become dependent on him to make her feel okay and loved, which is a set up for disaster right from the start. Like Cinderella, she may be moving from one prison to another. If I am talking to you, this book is designed to help you pause, reflect and analyze your life and the choices you have made. Most importantly, it is devoted to letting you know that you are not alone. A player's behaviors originate from something dysfunctional inside him, not from the mere myth that you are a "worthless" woman, as he may have you believe. You are worthy of love. Let us now learn how to choose differently when "man hunting."

Married Players and the Women that Worship Them reveals the essential qualities we must have in order to seek and hold love with an "honorable man." We will explore the direct correlations between your childhood years that have helped (you) create your present hell and your present situations. We will also examine the player's mind to understand why he behaves so badly.

If you are a wife who has been scorned by an unfaithful husband, you are probably living in your own hell. This book is most enlightening because it will help you transform your weaknesses into strengths and provide valuable information to help you make decisions that are in your own best interest. Most importantly, you will realize that you are not alone.

We will explore the concept of *happily ever after* and why we, as women, are wired to put up with bad behavior. As Shakespeare once wrote, "Hope springs eternal." You will learn to do away with *hope* and to put forth the action that gets you what you want in the long run. Once scorned, it so easy to sink

xviii   Married Players

into a black hole of negativity that makes you doubt yourself and all that surrounds you. This book explores the existential loneliness and the never ending introspection. What does it take to have a happy, faithful marriage? Do faithful men exist? I am happy to report that there are faithful men out there. You just need to know what to look for.

Secret Affairs and Secret Facts

While I composed this book, my goal was to make this information as straight-forward as possible. I wanted to make the connection between fantasy and reality, which are tied into the fairytale of yesterday and the destruction of today. It was not necessary to fill the pages with data and research that proves men are unfaithful because data is irrelevant. The relenting truth is that men screw around. It does not matter if seventy-five percent of the male population is players or if one-quarter of all men is unfaithful. One unfaithful man is far too many. Therefore, this book is for anyone who hurts, even the player who may find this book most enlightening and, perhaps, a real catalyst for change.

Note:

Throughout this book, subject names have been changed and scenarios have been altered to protect the privacy of those mentioned.

The Unfaithful Kingdom

Fie upon thy kingdom! He hast hurt many a woman. Why can't he just be faithful?

1

Cinderella's slipper

The most perfect union is when a handsome Prince courts the beautiful maiden and one year later they marry for *happily every after*. He loves her for the rest of their lives and continues to treat her like the love of his life; he never strays from her in any sense of the word. It is a perfect marriage made from a most perfect union of two soul mates while he takes care of her; he is committed to her in actions as well as words. They never squabble, argue or disagree because they are "perfect." *Happily ever after* would most likely mean a life without any problems or dilemmas. We can safely say this scenario is an unrealistic expectation of marriage that is doomed to fail right from the start.

Circles

When two people join together as one, they become a circle of unity. A marriage is when two individuals come together as one in partnership. When there is great love and compatibility between the partners, this "oneness" comes naturally. We do not seek to keep secrets from one another because this "other half" is the best friend that we have come to rely on a great deal. When we have too many differences, however, the circle begins to crack and shatter. There are reasons for this.

Marriage is difficult, if not impossible, for many people. Anyone who has been married understands that it takes a lot of time, commitment, and hard work to have a happy marriage. In order for couples to maintain the desire and devotion to one another, they must have a bond of partnership, and the happiest couples are compatible in many areas. The more compatible they are, the closer they are. They are best friends.

The saying *opposites attract* may be true, but how often do they stay "happily" together? How can you be truly happy with someone if you are constantly at opposite ends of the spectrum? Think about this for a moment. The strongest teams are those that are on the same side: a military unit is a band of brothers working together to defend against the outside enemy; a team of players bond as a unit by working together to compete against the opposing team. In marriage, happy couples work together toward common goals, interests and desires. If one partner wants a house in the mountains and the other by the beach, there is no common ground because one person has to compromise. If one partner wants six children and the other wants no children, there can be no compromise. You either have kids or you don't. Someone has to give up his or her "future" goals. Let us continue: If one person is a social butterfly and a night owl, while the other person is an early bird and a loner, where is the togetherness? Someone has to compromise by giving up who they are. It is bound to get irritating after a while because we tend to gravitate toward those who are most like us, and we tend to reject that which is most opposite of who we are. This is just human nature. We gravitate emotionally towards those who are similar to us because we seek to be understood and embraced.

Too often we overlook differences (when dating) and then charge right into a marriage that is doomed to fail. This is unfortunate because it generates so much pain that it destroys lives, careers and relationships. As strange as this may sound, the key to finding a soul mate is finding the courage to release that which is "not" love. No matter how much we try to deny it, we know in our hearts when a relationship is not working. We all may have experienced that painful nudge that tells us the love is gone. It is so difficult to let go of habits (that may be disguised as love) in order to make room for what may be the real thing some day. A large portion of this book is devoted to exploring how to do this. How do we let go of a habit and part from someone we like, admire, and respect, but are just not *in love with*? Most importantly, how do we know when we have finally found true love?

I was recently watching a documentary on Jewish marriage

and was interested to discover that the Jewish community has a lower divorce rate than any other. This is because of their simple dating rituals that appear to be very successful. They do not jump head over heals into relationships, but rather interview each other on short, formal dates in public places. This way they have no commitment to stay through a long dinner. The first meeting helps them evaluate their areas of compatibility. Are they similar people with similar desires? If they are compatible, they make plans for another date. It is important to note that they do not just jump in the sack on the first date either. They are seeking partners for life; the sex will come later. By all accounts, it looks like their process works wonders.

Too often we mistake physical attraction and lust for love. Whether or not we like it or are aware of this, the moment we go to bed with someone we become intimate. If we are incompatible in every other area but are compatible in bed, we run the risk of getting hooked on the sex. How can you give up something so good? There is a real conflict of interest because you may have a dead-end relationship with great sex. As time passes, the only things that may nudge the "relationship" to the *forever* level is an ultimatum of marriage or an accidental pregnancy. How can this be "happily ever after" when there is no compatibility or foundation that creates "partnership" in the marriage? When there is a lack of intimacy and friendship, the great sex eventually disappears.

Before we know it, we are living a lie. I like to refer to this as *manikin coupling*. By all appearances, they are the happy couple. He is the faithful husband and devoted father. He may very well love his wife, but there is an absence of mutual, intimate love. For the purpose of this book, we will say the husband finds his *happy ever after* outside the home and leads a double life (If we want to discuss unfaithful women, we need a separate book). This double life ends up creating havoc in all areas of his life: The wife is torn apart; the mistress is destroyed; his kids learn to live in a lie; he loses credibility with friends, and family members. It is a train wreck waiting to happen because deception is the deepest cut and drives people to do things they normally would not do.

No matter what our belief system, we can agree that infidelity generates an enormous amount of pain and has the possibility of provoking dangerous consequences. Although personal and religious beliefs sanction any form of infidelity, it is important to recognize that people are human. There are reasons people are unfaithful, and we will explore these reasons and the possible consequences that befall those who run around.

Society's Rules for Women

Oh, give to thee a *Scarlet Letter A* that I shall wear on my bosom to announce that I am a sinner who leads all men into temptation.

2

Unspoken Codes

Society has been forever forcing people to conform to a standard code of living. The unspoken rules of society have had profound influences on people by imposing negative consequences for "bad" behaviors. Various religious denominations impose "rules" with which some people may not be able to comply. In addition, our modernized age of technology makes it is easy for "dirty laundry" to be visible for all to see. This has resulted in some unthinkable, dangerous acts: suicide, homicide, or emotional/physical harm, and any other damage imaginable. If we do something "wrong," we may be exposed on any of the modernized internet sites or plastered all over the news. High profile figures know this all too well. The consequences are ruthless and there is no room for redemption nowadays.

Modern society may be more technologically advanced, but things are not too much different today than they were decades or centuries ago. The Puritan culture has always been unkind to those who commit adultery. For example, many perceive the mistress as a *bitch* who "steals" a married man- a woman who should be living in the everyday purgatory she "rightfully deserves," as many might see it. They should all run around with huge *A's* on their bosoms like Hester Prynne in Nathaniel Hawthorne's *The Scarlet Letter*. It would probably hurt a lot less.

It is also important to note that the wife of an unfaithful man hurts no less than our great-grandmothers had done years ago. Unfaithful men have always been "cads," and they are still less prone to suffer the consequences than women. It is the *Boys will be boys* kind of thing. An unfaithful husband is being a real jerk, but it is his mistress that has no brains or morals; his wife is "plain stupid" to stick with him. If all he gets is a *real jerk* label, then he is getting off pretty easy. Men take less of a hit than women.

Let's examine this point. Many of us have been in the lunch room when, for example, other people are gossiping about the affair Ellen (on the fifth floor) is having with Jake Doe, a married Service Representative (on the first floor). Here are some of the questions we might hear: How could she go with him when she knows he is married? Where are her morals? Does she realize he is just using her? I wondered what would happen if his wife found out? Doe she care that he is married with children? They may then, after decimating the *bitch mistress*, attack him by calling him a jerk or an *asshole* or someone so unscrupulous and unfit for humanity. The real culprit, however, is the other woman. She "stole" the married man and "lured" him into her web, forcing him to screw her. She ran after him, pinned him down and forced him to make love to her. Society has had one set of unspoken expectations for women and a different set of rules for men. Are the same questions asked if a single man is having an affair with a married woman? Is he called a "home wrecker" or a "manipulative bitch?" It is more likely that *boys will be boys*, or he is *getting while the getting is good*.

The truth of the matter is that you will not change public opinion, and you will not gain approval if you are coveting another woman's husband. People will gossip about you, discredit you, and you will be the ultimate loser; you may lose your career; your friends may disappear; family members may lose respect for you. The woman who messes with another's husband is the ultimate loser in some form or another.

Most surprisingly, women appear to be the harshest critics of other women who are messing around with married men. They may be afraid it will happen to them. I was shocked when a scandal erupted a few years back depicting a famous sportsman as a serious womanizer. It was a terrible scandal that continued for days. The media made good ratings berating this man, especially female commentators. It was then that I clearly saw the inequality and unfair treatment that I speak of now. Many female commentators displayed unrequited sentiments of anger and rage toward the women with whom this man had relations: He owes nothing to those trashy women because they are nothing but *cocktail waitress trash* and prostitutes or low-life trash with no morals whatsoever to whom he owes nothing. Much to my surprise and dismay, this woman did not utter one word that discussed this "player's" responsibility, or lack thereof. The perpetrator became the victim, and the victims were trashed in the eyes of society. Although many do not want to face reality, the truth is this man pursued these women with the intention of cultivating relationships with them. Not only did he use these women, but he made fools of them.

The sad point I want to make is that this man's situation is in no way a rare occurrence. It seems that lately there is such an epidemic of high-profile men committing unfaithful acts that I could write an entire book listing the names of unfaithful men; yet, society continues to persecute, destroy and pulverize the "other" women. These women are stuck in a world of pain before these "prince charmers" ride into their lives on fantasy horses but, after they are used and abused by these players, they are really stuck in a world of hurt.

Many would argue that these women put themselves in these situations because they knew what they are getting into. This is not necessarily so, especially if a woman has never been seduced by a married player before. These men may be such good con artists, as we will see, that they could talk any naïve woman into anything. I would also like to add that blame is irrelevant. What matters is that women wake up and smell the smoke before it burns down the house, metaphorically speaking.

If we want to have a rational discussion, it is wise to put blame aside and focus on enlightening women. If these men did not have female merchandise with whom to play, they would not be in control of the game. They would be out of business. As you will see as you read along, many mistresses are just as much victims as are the wives. The key is to expose the games these men play so that women "wake up" and avoid putting themselves in these situations. If players are unhappy in their marriages, tell them to get one of two things: a good marriage counselor or a good divorce attorney. Force them to shit or get off the pot, and do not let them play their unfaithful games like they have done since time began.

Beyond Society's Rules and into the Hearts of Women

There is also a large price a wife pays when she stays with a man that she knows is being unfaithful to her. She is the first one to know in her heart, but the last one to find out. She is perceived as a victim, especially if she has children, and she may be looked upon as a fool. Society demonizes her for taking him back after he has messed around on her a few times. The famous nagging questions haunt her: Why did he cheat on her? What about her didn't he want? Perhaps she drove him to run around on her. This has a profound affect on her self worth and forces her to either leave him or stay with him, but either way there is a stigma attached. Divorce is a bad word, especially if there are kids involved. Reconciliation comes with a price, as panic and fear forever remain when she takes him back. How can she ever trust him when he has proven himself untrustworthy? There is no peace for the weary.

Please Pass the Bread Pan

My grandmother was a fabulous cook and baker. I once asked her numerous questions about baking and cooking, and she was happy to pass on her information. While showing me how to make bread, she directed me to use the old, stainless steel "rectangular" pan. No other pan would produce the same results! When I got a little older, I realized that my grandmother was very poor in her early years and an "old, stainless steel" bread pan was all that was available to her at that time. I realized that the taste of the bread had nothing to do with the depth, width or texture of the pan. It was rather a handed-down, generational directive on *how the poor bake bread in a borrowed pan from the neighbor.* She had seen her mother bake bread in this pan and, since the bread baked so well and tasted so good, she continued the routine. It became a family tradition.

These types of handed-down customs are with us all the time. We are all products of our environment and have been "trained" by our ancestors to repeat the patterns of living as they had done. When it comes to mating rituals, we learned all

the rules from our mothers, grandmothers, and great-
grandmothers who taught us how to be women.

For centuries women have been fighting for equal rights,
liberation and equality, and we still continue to fight. If we
study history and are well-aware of what our females ancestors
went through, however, we can understand why they fought so
hard. Our female ancestors had lived in worlds of denial and,
back in the day, it was not common for couples to communicate
about intimacy issues. Men and women simply did not talk
about "deep" things, just like Ricky and Lucy Ricardo did not
sleep in the same bed during the 1950's comedy *I Love Lucy*. The
word pregnancy was not acceptable on television. "In a family
way" was more like it. If a young, unmarried woman was
pregnant, she was just a young girl *in trouble*.

Society has always imposed unspoken rules and codes that
dictate the way people should relate to one another. For
example, if a single woman became pregnant years ago, she was
ridiculed or looked down upon, and her family may have
disowned her or shipped her off to boarding school somewhere
far away. Moreover, if a man got a woman pregnant back then,
he was almost always forced to marry her because she needed a
man to take care of her. What did this do for the *happily ever after*
in many marriages? A forced or expected marriage almost
always turns out poorly, especially for the woman. Let us
explore this concept for a moment because it is worth noting the

pain and destruction to which the rules of society have contributed.

During the Puritan days, for example, people were burned at the stake if they acted contrary to the rules of society. It was the purpose of the Puritan predilection to control the population and give them tenets for acceptable behaviors; therefore, they had strict sexual standards during this time. Society had a jaundice view of extra marital affairs. Infidelity gave cause for beheading in the gallows while the onlookers chanted. This was much more serious than gossip because it was considered a violation of community standards. If a single woman was caught in a compromising position with a man, for example, there was no where for her to run and hide. Nothing was going to save her from the ruthless spectators while society scoffed at her "despicable" behavior.

Further, in Civil War times, it was expected that a young lady be a virgin on her wedding night, but the man, however, was expected to be sexually experienced. He would venture to the "lower class" part of town to court a woman he deemed suitable, play with her for a while and then return back to his middle class fiancé. It is important to note that a young woman born into lower class had the hope of finding a middle class man to save her from poverty, much like wishing the handsome Prince would ride in on his horse to save poor Cinderella.

In the 1950's, relationships between husbands and wives

were often void of emotional intimacy. It was uncommon for men and women to share feelings with one another because they had not been taught to be open and "intimate." They were sexually and emotionally repressed. This was part of the reason for the seed that planted the Woodstock generation. Women were much more submissive to men back then. The misses took care of the home, and her "faithful" husband worked to bring home a paycheck. Girls were not expected to have career goals, but were rather expected to walk down the isle to become wife and mother. Her purpose was to be a homemaker. Men were, therefore, expected to find a nice girl, get married and stay happily married. This was the *Ozzie and Harriet* syndrome (sitcom, The Adventures of Ozzie and Harriet, 1952), as I call it. Although infidelity was often ignored and shoved under the rug back then, it was just as prevalent as it is today, if not more.

Our ancestors were set up for failure. Think about this for a moment. How can we expect kids to know what they want for the moment, never mind happily ever after for the rest of their lives? The answer would be no different back then, only it was expected at that time. They were not mature enough to know what they wanted in life. How could they promise to stay faithful forever when they had no clue what forever was? If divorce was shunned, as it often was, they avoided it at all costs. Consequently, men grabbed their happiness on the side, and women buried their heads in the sand as long as they were taken care of financially. This was a learned pattern of behavior. Their kids, therefore, were raised in families that did not openly show affection and love. There was an unspoken language of dysfunction that was handed down through the generation branches. Consequently, they created a rebellious generation that rejected the taboos of societal mores. This point is exemplified in *Rebel Without A Cause* (1955), starring James Dean, the movie that many parents forbade their children to watch.

We all remember or have heard of the liberation in the 1960's when the kids of the early fifties matured, like wild animals sprung from cages, prompting sexual, emotional and financial liberation. They were busting out of their parents "repression." Women also explored swinging with various partners and open marital sex, as they revolted against their mothers' frigid and obedient belief system. Society, especially the older generation of women, were outraged by this movement. They were appalled at the "young girls these days," as my grandmother once commented. Although I was just a child during this time, I can remember the condemnation that my grandmother had toward the younger generation of females.

Inside the Mistress Prison

In all my life, I have never felt like such a worthless object that had no real entitlement to anything, especially the truth.

3

Rapunzel

Before I begin our tour of mistress prison, I would like to say that there are reasons we get involved with married men. It isn't as though we woke up one morning and said, "I am going to find some woman's husband, have a sexual affair with him so I can be used, abused and treated like a worthless, inanimate object." In most cases, it is actually a slow process, like being sucked under a tidal wave. Before we know it, we are drowning. We will discuss how we get ourselves trapped in this prison of hell.

I will begin by offering a word of caution. If you have just met a married man and are contemplating having an affair with him, don't do it. Don't put yourself in harm's way because it might be the most painful experience you have ever had, and it will be next to impossible to escape. As much as you say you will not get emotionally involved, the chances are likely that you will. Once we have intimate relations with men, we become attached. Remember that he has a wife, and statistics prove that ninety-percent of the time he will not leave her for anyone, including you. These men have the skilled ability of conning you for their own interests.

If, however, you have been involved with a married man and are desperately trying to get a commitment from him, know that you may or may not get it. This book will help you examine your situation and provide tools to help you make decisions. If you are trying to break free of the mistress chains, it will be tougher if you do not have a support network. It helps if you date other "single" men. However, if you go out on a date with one man and it is a disaster, you may run back to your married lover. You might want to set up a situation where you have three or four dates lined up so that you will not be left with a hopeless feeling if one does not pan out. Keep your options open.

Being in love with a married man can blindly deplete your self worth because the more involved you become, the less he may give you. The admiration and attention he gave when he was courting you may begin to dissipate when he knows he has you hooked. You are second fiddle and will most likely take a back seat to his wife. After he leaves your bedroom, he will run back to his wife and may not contact you for a few days. Once you get close to him again, he will most likely abandon you yet another time. She comes first, and this will take a direct toll on your self worth after a while. Resentment will set in and a

worthless feeling will come your way. The goal is to find
yourself again because you need to feel as attractive, worthy,
and alive as you used to feel. If you are in this situation because
you have always lacked self worth, then we need to get you to
the point where you have self worth.

On the other hand, some women prefer to remain mistresses
because they do not want committed relationships. They prefer
the attention, the sex, the friendship, or a quasi-relationship that
requires no investment. If this is the case and you do not put
yourself in a situation where you have much to lose, then you
will not risk as much. If nothing else, this book will impart
knowledge and help you understand yourself more clearly.

If, however, you want a husband and have fallen deeply in
love with a married man that has said he will not leave his wife,
then you are setting yourself up for an emotional crash. No
amount of love, sex, or friendship will ever lure a married man
away from his wife if he wants to stay married to her. This
could be a dangerous situation if you have not clearly defined
your wants, needs and future goals. Most importantly, if you
have not looked at your situation in total reality, you might be
sucked into a fantasy that could ultimately drive you to do the
unthinkable acts that have ruined so many lives in the past.

Define your situation. Look at it from the point of reality.
Explore the ramifications of what you are doing. Does this
situation work for you the way it is? Are you happy and

complete with your situation?

If we think about this realistically, infidelity brings enormous moral and social judgments and ramifications. He is being unfaithful to a woman with whom he made religious and moral vows, and you are the other woman. Does he harbor guilt for hurting his wife and children, should there be kids involved? Does he harbor guilt for holding onto you when he knows he is not giving you a "real" relationship? These are painful questions the "other woman" avoids many times. Guilt is a toxic emotion and has a way of eating into relationships like cancerous cells. A healthy relationship cannot survive without total honesty, trust and commitment. This is something to think about should you end up with your married lover on a permanent basis someday.

Inside the Mistress Prison

If you are a woman in love with a married man and view him as more than just an affair, life is difficult for you. Ninety-percent of the time you spend your life without him. As in any intimate relationship, you feel as though a part of you is missing in his absence. However, his commitment is to his wife, not you. Until he makes the decision to ask his wife for a divorce and makes a commitment to you, you are only having an affair with him. This fact generates so much pain, loneliness, anger, and resentment. No matter what the feeling, you constantly feel the same "part of you is missing" as you would if he were yours. It is a roller coaster ride because your emotions fluctuate. Further, he is in total control of your "relationship," and his schedule determines when you will see him again. This puts pressure on you because you must plan your life around the events that take place in his life. This is not an equal relationship with equal power. You are at his mercy.

Think about this for a second. If you are a mistress, you think that you are the only one in his heart because he cultivates a fantasy world with you, but you are far from the only woman. It hurts. Friday nights are empty. The weekends are empty. You try to fill your time by doing what you want to do and what you have to do, but there is a part of you missing. He is with his wife and family instead of being with you. Your mind begins to perseverate because you know that you are missing out on a "real" relationship, especially when you see husbands and wives shopping together. By Sunday night you become very resentful of his wife and kids. You feel you are nothing but a hidden secret, a toy for him to play with when he feels like it. You still do not have a ring, commitment, or anything other than promises of someday that never comes. On Monday morning it disappears, and then he calls again with plans to see you this week. You now have something to which you can look forward. In five days another weekend will arrive. Before you know it, three years have slipped by, and then ten.

Therefore, if society wishes to impose judgment and

punishment upon the "mistress whore," then let the Scarlet Letter *A* be second option. She is already in purgatory.

The Princess is Lost

The consequences of the mistress prison can cause serious emotional distress. It is a roller coaster ride and the speed, height and velocity depend on his life at home. Literally, the mistress is lost. She is enthralled in a secret affair that dictates her life. As with all addictions, she loses parts of her life forever.

The mistress is involved in an unstable, insecure affair that becomes her relationship. Half the time she does not know what is happening or what is going to happen because whatever she gets from him depends on the extra time he takes from other areas in his life. Instead of spending a life together, she may get three hours on Wednesday night or five hours on Thursday, if he can play hooky from work. It is an unstable situation that invokes erratic emotions. This may affect every area of her life: She may lose touch with friends or family for certain lengths of time; she may lose her interest, passions and goals; her job may be affected.

The player, however, is unconscious to the pain he causes his mistress because he refuses to take action and, in most cases, will not tell the truth to his wife. He wants to have his cake and eat it too, all while hiding behind his kids in most cases. The player says he cannot leave his children and talks about all the years his wife has given him. He may feel platonic love for his wife and, at the same time, feel tremendous guilt because she is in love with him. Interestingly enough, he cannot face the sad truth that even though he is not in love with his wife, he does not want her with another man. It is the *Tarzan territory* thing, when the thought of another man in his territory makes him upset. Should his wife distance herself and make him jealous, he may freak out because she is his territory. Even if he does not want her, he will not have another man taking his wife away from him. Further, he definitely will not tolerate another man becoming a stepfather to his children. It is a subconscious territorial thing which men have that is, I must say, very selfish and misleading. It is a natural assumption to believe if a man is jealous, he must be in love. Not so. He may just not want another man invading his territory. Consequently, his wife mistakes his jealousy for love. This deception ruins many lives, especially the kids, because he is living a lie and is promoting false hope of reviving an *already dead relationship*.

Princess Profile

To recapitulate, women do not wake up one morning and say I am going to choose a married man so he can use me, hurt me, treat me like his toy, and then abandon me over and over again. Most mistresses are not married men chasers. Surprisingly enough, many are reserved women who have solid morals (as society would judge). Many are reserved and lonely, which are the very features that attract these predators to them.

Consequently, these women are susceptible to the charm, adulation and attention that these men generously shower.

If we understand why some women choose to get involved with married men, we will not be so quick to judge them. I have met many women who were either having or have had affairs with married men and most of them say that the affair "just happened." It was not planned. In fact, they said it was not something they wanted. Most said they only had one affair and would never do it again. Some were bitter because they felt used and tossed aside, but most were grateful because the affair helped them decide what they wanted in a "real" relationship and what they wanted in a man. I am only aware of one man who left his wife for her. Although this may happen, it appears to be a rare occurrence because men want to play on the side without upsetting their secure worlds at home.

In an effort to find answers, I made a list of common traits that these women shared. We could call it a mistress profile or a list of common characteristics that demonstrates their vulnerability to putting themselves in mistress prisons.

The most common trait I noticed was that mistresses were emotionally insecure and had a deep-seated fear of intimacy. They had a history of poor relationships; they seemed to choose men who were unavailable and had abandoned them in some form or another. Mistresses may also find these affairs safer because if does not work out with the married one, it is not a direct rejection because he was already taken. This is a direct correlation to their childhoods, where either their mothers or fathers were not available. Consequently, they suffered the effects of unstable relationships and found it difficult to depend on someone to meet their needs. Deep-seated trust issues arose because they suffered from neglect, and there was also some form of abuse: physical, sexual, emotional or mental. Their confidence had been tested time and again, and their happiness was dependent upon someone loving them. As a result, they have become desirable to married men who know how to glamorize them and put them on pedestals. Players make them feel unrealistically wonderful and special, which generates a false feeling of worthiness.

If a woman is in this situation, she may want to think about where the road is taking her. If I am talking to you, the best thing you can do is watch what he does. Are his actions consistent with his rhetoric? Married men may build up your confidence and make you feel one-hundred feet tall. In a sense, you become the most beautiful, intelligent, and desirable woman in the world, which is euphoric for the woman who has been neglected and deprived. Euphoria is like a drug high with which you may find it impossible to live without. It is the all-time dopamine rush. Everything you have ever needed and wanted has come in his nice, little package, but you eventually see, as we will discuss later, that it is just that, a package. The danger is that this relationship gives you permission to avoid resolving your childhood issues. You may get stuck in a nice, comfortable love affair that is going nowhere. This is mistress prison.

I must stress that everyone has a different story. These are just some common traits that may or may not apply to you. However, there are reasons you are in an affair rather than a fulfilling relationship and, again, it depends on what you want. Let us now explore some options.

If you have a pen and paper handy, create your own profile now. Draw one vertical line down the center of the paper. On the left side of the paper, make a list of the wonderful things about your married lover. List all the positive adjectives that describe how he makes you feel. Now on the right side, list the negative ways he makes you feel. Turn to the left side of the back of the paper now and make a list of things you wish you had when you were a child. Now move to the right side and make a list of the adjectives that describe how your caretaker made you feel as a child. Examine both columns. You should see some similarities between your current situation and your childhood relationships. Information is power that generates enlightenment.

We can take this exercise one step further. On another sheet of paper, make a list of all the things you desire: What do you want for your future? Ask yourself if you are currently in a situation that will help you obtain your future goals. If the answer is no, then explore your fears. What are you afraid of? What is holding you back? List them as they come to mind. Although this is a very painful exercise, it is worth the pain. Our goal is to find peace, happiness and fulfillment. Only you can determine what is right for you.

Tears of a Queen

Oh, how she cries herself to sleep. If only he were hers to keep.

4

The Wife Revealed

It may seem so unfair and down right cruel to speak of the other woman's pain when the one being harmed is his wife. I am in no way minimizing or negating the wife's torment. One of the most painful experiences for any woman is that she finds out that her husband is cheating on her. This is the most hurtful, deceptive and painful experience she could ever encounter. She is dead to the world (emotionally) and is consumed with so many negative emotions that she can hardly breathe, let alone function. To exacerbate the situation, if she finds out he has had many lovers, she really feels had, like a first class fool. This is a dangerous situation for all parties, especially if there are kids involved. Unfortunately, somewhere in her subconscious she has known the truth for quite some time. She has probably lived in a world of denial, ignoring the red flags that came her way but had such a need to believe in this man that she slipped into denial. Once the truth is discovered, however, her mind becomes a race car engine, roaring and speeding with memories that she can neither control nor explain. She becomes unstable and erratic. Memories flood her mind and keep reeling with no end in sight. There is nothing that can comfort her or make the truth less painful. She has no choice but to accept the reality that she tried to keep at bay for so long.

When she reaches back into the *history keeper* of her mind, she can remember that his first wife once told her that he was unfaithful in his first marriage, or that his ex-girlfriend once warned her that he is an unfaithful man. She may remember that he was very hesitant right before their wedding day and almost backed out at the last minute. She may remember that she had to chase after him for a few months before she became pregnant with their first child, the child that brought their marriage together. She thinks about the flirtatious look he gave the waitress when they went to dinner three months ago. She may also remember the conference to which he attended out of state last year-the conference at the hotel where she could not reach him. She might think back to his time in the computer room three weeks ago when he changed the screen abruptly as soon as she walked into the room.

When she finally composes herself, she will ask the question: "How could he do this to me?" This is the standard question that screams from her inner core. We will discuss why he does this (to you) in the coming chapters. The most important thing to grasp is that he did not do this to you. He would have "done this" to any woman he was with because he is a dishonest man. You may have some things to learn, but the fact is that he was the one who made the choice to be deceptive, not you.

The Wife in the Mirror

After the storm has passed and reality surfaces, it is natural for a wife to feel like there is something inherently wrong with her. Perhaps she was not good enough for him, or she was not enough of a woman to keep him. The feelings of worthlessness and emptiness are overwhelming. She begins to reflect on herself and her life with him. Sometimes she may become so desperate that she does unthinkable things that are destructive and hurtful. She may attack her husband or attempt to kill him or may plan to approach and attack the mistress. A scorned wife may find a lawyer and sue the mistress for Alienation of Affection, given she lives in a state that holds current law. She may even plan to find a man and have sex with a stranger to indulge in self destructive behavior: "If my husband does not want me, then someone else will." She may plan revenge and try to take her husband for all he is worth financially. There was a case in the newspaper not to long ago where a scorned wife made her husband stand on the street corner and wear a sign stating he had been unfaithful. An unfaithful player can certainly make a wife crazy and, consequently, she may do crazy things.

If you are a scorned wife, let us take a brief time out from your *black hole* of pain. Let's get you grounded and stable again. If you do anything in haste, you will only hurt yourself. You have been through enough pain.

Hold Your Horses

If you watch someone react in the most stressful situations, this gives you an idea of who they are at the core because a person's true character surfaces in dire straights. No matter what is done to us or how badly we may get screwed over, we are still responsible for our own actions. For example, if you decide to kill a woman because you believe she "stole" your man, then you will suffer the consequences in prison for the rest of your life. Is it worth it? Is he worth it? Put these irrational thoughts to the side for now.

Just as a mistress has a profile with distinct traits that lead her into the arms of a married player, the wife of a player also has traits that lead her down the isle to the arms of a philanderer. Her background may be similar to that of the mistress. She may have come from a dysfunctional family setting where there was a need to escape the harsh reality around her. It could have been alcohol related or some other form of discomfort.

Children that are reared in chaotic, unstable homes find any means to escape reality. They find fantasy worlds or other means to pretend that things are not so bad. Further, if a child is physically abused by a parent, the child may beg to stay with the abuser in the threat of being taken away. If the parent is physically abusive to the child and then turns right around and apologizes, the youngster will have conflicting emotions. The child will most likely pretend that everything is wonderful and beg to stay in the environment at all costs.

This is especially true for adult children of alcoholics who were not given the chance to live in reality. Let us explore this further. I prefer to use this example because it is easy to understand. Let us say that the parent fluctuated back and forth from intoxication to sobriety, leaving the poor child confused about what true reality was at the moment. Consequently, the child learned to adapt to the parent's different worlds of reality: one when the parent was intoxicated and one when the parent was sober. The child was left to figure out what reality existed from moment to moment. This is very difficult for a young girl and has a profound affect on her future relationships. With no real example of stability, she may struggle the rest of her life to figure out what is real in her relationships. The young lady will most likely have trust or abandonment issues and may be desperate for stability and security. She someday ends up with an unfaithful husband and uses her familiar skills of denying reality and pretending that everything is wonderful.

If a single woman (as this) chooses an unstable man who will run around on her, she may avoid all signs of his abusive behavior. Instead of being turned off by this, like the stable woman who came from a stable environment, she may chase after him. She marries him and continues to live in a fantasy world, pretending to herself that whatever she is seeing is not real. Unfortunately, she repeats the childhood cycle with a mate this time instead of a parent.

Let us say that Cathy is planning to go on a date to the movies with a guy named Stanley. She is smitten with him and is excited that he asked her out. She is so nervous and giddy that she cannot even focus on the first hour of the movie. She wonders if her hair looks perfect and if he is smitten with her. The woman focuses so much on Stanley and whether or not he likes her that she is not emotionally free to notice him. Since she misses the first half of the movie, she cannot fully grasp what is happening in conclusion of the story. It is ironic that she missed the important scenes that lead up to the climax and conclusion to the storyline. This is symbolic of her relationship and may foreshadow that which is to come in her marriage.

She eventually marries Stanley and finds out years later he has been unfaithful to her with numerous women. When she looks back at this very first date, she realizes that she was so preoccupied with the inadequacies in herself that she could not see the inadequacies in Stanley when he left to use the restroom three times and was on his cell phone. She missed the first half of the storyline with Stanley which told her the truth about who he was. Consequently she never understood the movie and she never understood Stanley. Cathy had to see what she needed to see. This is indicative of insecure women that have a driving need to be wanted and loved. Cathy, for example, focused too much on whether or not Stanley liked her and did not even contemplate whether or not Stanley was worthy of her love.

I once had a very close family member through marriage that I will call Cara. Cara was married to Harry for sixteen years, and I was under the impression that her marriage had been wonderful. One day she called me in hysteria claiming that she finally caught Harry with a secret cell phone and then followed him to his mistress's home. She flew into a dangerous rage, breaking things in a nuclear fit of aggression. When the storm finally passed, she admitted that she was relieved because she did not have to pretend any longer. This experience had forced her to confront the truth. She saw all the signs throughout the years, but she made him lie to her; she desperately needed the excuses. It was a convenient set up so that she could continue to keep face and stay in a dead-end marriage because she feared being alone.

The Wife's Empty Castle

If you do not know what you are getting into, then how can you plan your way out? If you don't know the truth, then how do you know what the lies are? These are questions that women need to ask themselves before they venture into a lifelong commitment with a man. Think about this for a moment. When you walk into a building, you always know the way out. It is a subconscious thing. You go out the way you came in. What if, however, the exit was not visible and you entered in a one-way section of the establishment? The first thing you would do (subconsciously) is look around for the exit. It is an instinctive protective measure; it is human nature. If women applied this principle to dating, they would not end up in the meat grinder.

Women too often will buy a car without examining the motor or other critical aspects of a car. If he is a good salesman, he can talk you into anything. Women need to look beyond the words and do research on their own. Otherwise, they will end up in empty castles with broken dreams.

An unhappily married woman can be spotted for miles. Her facial expressions and body language tell her story to the world. When she is with an unfaithful man, she carries the existential loneliness and panic in every part of her body. She may pretend she has the June Clever household, but what is her life really like when she cannot find her husband half of the time and is forever chasing after his love? This woman lives in a world of insecurity and fear. Given the situation, she feels unworthy of his love and feels she is competing with other women for his attention. If she is with a player, she is most certainly sitting on the sidelines while he is running around. This destroys her self esteem and damages her relationship with her kids. She has zero tolerance and the smallest things will set her off. She is temperamental, agitated and frustrated, much like having emotional blue balls with lingering pain. It becomes a dangerous obsession. She is constantly exhausted from expending energy, analyzing his behaviors and seeking evidence that she hopes she will not find. She searches for anything that will prove her wrong, anything that will give her permission to stay with him. She desperately longs to be loved, but she senses in her gut that her husband does not want her. She knows he is not in love with her. He may not touch her or talk to her or take interest in her. She feels dead on the inside as she tries to go through the motions of motherhood every day. The thought that he may go off with another woman terrifies her. It is absolute hell.

More importantly, a woman pays a high price for marrying a man that she knew ahead of time would be unfaithful to her. She is angry at herself because she made the decision to marry him, even though she knew the truth.

The choices we make dictate the lives we will lead. Watch him and the movie next time, not yourself. Be confident in who you are and what you have to offer, all while examining every aspect about him. Decide if you want to buy the car, not if he wants to sell it to you.

Before the Castle

If a single woman knows in her heart that her man flirts with other women and, perhaps, comes across actual evidence that he may have someone else, the worst thing she can do is give him an ultimatum of marriage. If she says, "We've been together for two years now and we either end it or get married," she is setting herself up for a lifetime of pain. She thinks that if he agrees to marry her, this will prove that he loves her more than all other women. This is not necessarily the case. Once a cheater, always a cheater, and there are only a few exceptions to the rule that we will discuss later on.

I once had a good friend, Kate, who told me the painful history of her courting years and eventual marriage to John. After a few years of courting, she noticed John was acting strangely and decided to pop up at his house, where she found him in bed with the neighbor. Kate flew into a rage and then left him in a manipulative ploy to punish him. He was full of apologetic words and begged her not to leave him. A few days later she softened up and took him back. "That's it! We either get married or I am moving away and we are done!" They married in the 1970's and had a few kids.

Ten years later, however, her best friend was staying at their home. Kate just happened to awaken during the night to use the restroom. She heard noises coming from the living room, ventured down the hall and found her best friend in a compromising position with John on the recliner chair. Although she said she did not catch them doing anything, she knew they had done something. As a result, she evicted her "best" friend and confronted him, but he denied any wrong doing. Kate stayed with him and, in fact, is still with him until this day. The sad fact is that she is always looking over her shoulder with heart-wrenching insecurity that robs her of peace.

No matter what your situation, if you do not accept the reality of what you see beforehand, you will spend a lifetime of hell expending energy forcing him to be faithful to you. If he is not faithful now, then he will definitely not be faithful if you coerce him to marry you.

The hardest thing for many women to do is to let go of a man. If he is showing you that he is just not that into you, then he is not going to be that much more into you if you manipulate, force or trap him into marriage. Most importantly, you hurt yourself by hanging onto him because you waste precious time; you are wasting your youthful years and the good guys will slip away. The question, however, still remains: Why would you want a man that does not want you? We will explore this question in later chapters, but it all has to do with self worth and conditioning. You do not want to be the kind of woman that keeps hanging on. Think about this for a moment. Society conditions us from the time we are little girls that we are worthy if we have a man. Little girls play with dolls and pretend they are wives and mommies. Bigger girls seek boyfriends and have cat fights with other girls they believe are "after" their boyfriends. College girls will (many times) put their boyfriends before their studies. By the time they are in their mid-to- late twenties, many women become desperate for marriage and babies. If they are unmarried in their thirties, women become desperate because their biological clocks are ticking away; they may panic and extend ultimatums to their boyfriends to "rope" them into marriage. Unfortunately, women have been conditioned that they are not "normal" without mates. We are conditioned at a young age that we should do as our great-grandmothers have done: get married and make babies.

The first step is to recognize this subconscious conditioning. You must first learn to love yourself. How do you expect a man to love you if you do not love yourself? You teach a man how to treat you by the way you treat yourself and by the boundaries you set for him.

If you have come from a dysfunctional home and were deprived of your basic hierarchical needs, then you may need some professional help. A trained professional, therapist, may help you uncover the demonstrative demons from your past that have helped you choose the wrong men and attract abusive situations. If you bring to your therapist the inventory sheet you completed a while back, he or she may put you on the right path to emotional wellness. You must first uncover your childhood traumas so that you stop depending on a man and become your own first love.

The next step is to start thinking as an "honorable" man thinks. Men are concerned with survival and productivity. They charge through life and figure ways to manipulate their surroundings, not people. Notice those two words: *manipulate* and *surroundings*. Women are more prone to manipulate *situations* and *people*. I once knew a wise woman who made me smile with two key points about men: "All men think about is their wallets and their dicks. And if you count on a man for emotional support, he is good for about a half an hour. Then he is as useless as a burned out light bulb." Although this may seem like "male bashing," there is an element of truth to it. Let us put it in logical terms that are more constructive and a bit complementary.

A man strives to produce, both financially and reproductively. He needs to make money to support a family, and he needs the sperm to create a family. This is how his chemical wiring is designed. He is wired to flood the gene pool. We will discuss this more in closing chapters. He is also a fixer, a solution finder, and does not get sucked into the emotional drama as do women. He wants to quickly find a solution to a problem and move on. It frustrates him when a woman repeatedly "whines" about the same thing because he feels he can't fix it for her. If you think like a man thinks, you will have less of an emotional dependence and more of a peaceful autonomy.

With all this being said, do as men do: Think of your own productivity first, and then seek a partner to stand by your side—a man who has the same passion as you. If you want to find a good husband, you must first find a good man. I should say find the "right man," as we discussed at the beginning of this book. Once you learn to love yourself, you will begin to protect yourself better and will then attract a good man. And you will avoid becoming intimately involved with a man that is going to stomp in your garden and piss on your flowers, pardon my fiendish language. You will not allow a "jerk" to walk all over you like a door mat. Most importantly, you won't give yourself away to an abusive situation of any kind, whether it be wife or mistress. You will be able to slip on those high boots in a huge pile of cow manure and run like hell.

Unfortunately, women waste far too much time in dead-end relationships. Therefore, focus on yourself and learn to identify the conditioning in your mind. Clean out your childhood closets and find out who and what you are. Once you find interests, goals, dreams, passions, you will then attract a man who shares common interests. If you find a compatible mate, you have a better chance of finding a best friend who will not stray.

The Prince's Profile

Tell me more, Fair Lover, for you are my
Knight in shining armor that has come to my
emotional rescue.

5

Let us begin by noting that not all married men are players. If you are a wife, you may have a situation where your husband has not been a predatory player and has not made a fool of you, but rather the two of you grew apart, and (unfortunately) he fell in love with someone else. He may be an otherwise honest, honorable man that did not want to hurt you and did not know what to do. He may spend the rest of his days seeking atonement that may never come. Perhaps both of you have grown apart and aspired for different goals, and maybe you did not want to accept reality. If this is the case, your experiences will be less painful than if you have been married to a predatory player. Use your experience to your advantage and learn from it. We grow from the pain in the darkness, much like mushrooms grow from no light. The goal is to travel through the darkness and into the light of true peace and happiness.

If you are a mistress, you may be involved with an honest, otherwise faithful man that just happened to fall in love with you and has no clue what to do about it, especially if he has kids. This type of relationship is a lot less painful on a deeper level because at least you know his love for you is genuine, only bound by circumstances. If you are involved with a married player, however, it can be excruciating because his love may not be genuine although it appears to be. This is when you feel like a *piece of ass*, which is *dewomanizing* as well as dehumanizing.

No matter what your situation, it is hell when you are in love with a man who is not committing to you and, since he is living a double life, everything he says is suspect. How can you trust him? It is like you are living in the twilight zone trying to figure out what is real and what is false with him. You eventually see and feel how unstable the situation is and only those who have gone through similar situations can fully understand what you are going through. You feel compelled to find out if he is just using you, if he really loves you or if he is just *bullshitting* you for his own selfish gain.

The first thing we must do is distinguish the unfaithful wimps from the predatory players. It is extremely important that you see the difference.

The Unfaithful Wimp

While I was writing this book, I had a difficult time creating a subtitle for this section. I searched my mind and the parallel universe for an alternate title to *wimp*, but I was unable to finding anything that compares. Let us define this term.

A wimp is someone who lacks the balls to stand up for truth

and lacks the courage to make decisions. For the purpose of our conversation, we will say that the wimp is a man who is overwhelmed by guilt, fear or some form of manipulation that interferes with his ability to act on the *honest* principle. In relevance to this book, we can say that the unfaithful wimp does not have enough balls to leave the woman he is not *in love with*.

At the same time, please know I am not advocating divorce or that men leave their wives. What I am suggesting, however, is that men live by honor and make choices that are rooted in reality and truth. There is no greater insult to a woman than to have a man play the part of a "dutiful" husband. If he is not in love with his wife and has fallen madly in love with another woman, then he should tell the truth, no matter how painful-- no matter who it hurts. Deceptions are more painful than any truth. No wife wants to lie next to a man in bed when he has recently stuck his penis in another woman's vagina.

If we fall into the debate of how he should not have gotten involved with somebody else to begin with, we can revert back to the term wimp once again. He made *wimpy* choices in his life for which he may now be paying, and this we will discuss shortly. We also fall into the trap of having a moral debate, which once again evokes religious and moral sanctions. Our goal, again, is to help transform through enlightenment, not condemnation. With all that being said, a wimp is defined as a man that will not stand up for the absolute truth.

A wimp is anyone who will not stand up for the truth all while continuing to live a lie. You may very well be involved with a man who sincerely loves you and has never had an affair (on his wife) in the past. All of the sudden he meets you and is clueless as to what to do. If he has spent years with his wife and has kids with her, he may very well love her. He meets you and realizes you are the one woman he has waited for his whole life. This scares the hell out of him, if I may speak frankly once again. You, however, are the love of his life, and he finds himself in constant turmoil. He is an emotional wreck, riddled with guilt, self-loathing and a fear that God or some higher power is going to drag him to the darkest purgatory in hell. If this is the case, it will be a lot easier for you to get what you want in the long run because you will not be digging and fishing for answers all over the place. Unlike the married player, this man cannot compartmentalize and squeeze you into a pillar (as we will discuss shortly), nor does he know how to manipulate, connive and put his feelings in a box. He is much more impulsive and neurotic. Chances are, this affair will not last very long because he does not have the deceptive character to keep it going and, eventually, will implode, explode or confess. All of these options will force change of some kind. He may experience tremendous guilt about what he is doing, and this is a good sign that he is not merely a player using you for a *piece of ass*.

No matter what, he is still married to another woman, and

you have to decide if you want to remain in the closet for the remainder of your youthful years. If he is a real religious man with a large religious family, chances are you will not win. God always prevails with these men and their vows will remain in tact. After he ends it with you, he may very well "repent" and renew his vows with his wife out of guilt.

If you are the wife married to a wimp, you may want to use this experience for inner personal growth and work together to put your marriage back together. You may very well have a good, decent man, but you will need to decide if you want to take him back. Perhaps you need the deep love you share together, or you may need to take him back because of the kids and all the years you have had together. You may also decide to let him go if he truly is in love with another woman. Do you want a man who is in love with another woman? Do you want to free yourself so that you may find a man who truly loves you? Some women prefer to stay together at all costs because the fear of change and fear of being alone is too great. Consequently, they miss out on "real" love. This is typical of high school sweethearts who have spent twenty-five years together and are afraid of change; they work tirelessly to fall back in love or rekindle a flame that burned out long ago.

Player Defined

The predatory player is the man that hides behind the creation of this book. This is a hard-core player that is the worst nightmare we can imagine. Unfortunately, too many women fall victim to these men. This is the wolf in sheep clothing or the *Car Salesman* type of man. By definition, he is the ultimate wrecking ball that heads right for you and destroys your entire life. As one man stated, "Women are so dumb when it comes to men. I can con my way into any pair of underwear and can manipulate, connive, charm and get exactly what I want. They need to wake up and stop being so stupid." The truth is that women are not stupid. We just see through different color glasses because our needs are different than those of men.

The danger with this type of man is that we cannot see him coming; we cannot even see him standing before us many times. He hides behind a mask of innocence, charm, honesty, and sincerity, all while he is calculating his next move. His mannerisms flourish with inviting charm and, unfortunately, the only way to spot this type of man is to watch his behavior over a period time. If we listen to what he does and ignore what he says, the red flag warning signs will be waving so fast that we cannot deny them.

One way to avoid this type of man is to make sure you have created (within you) a boundary wall that detects the warning signs. When we are raised in supportive, loving environments, our parents teach us (when we are young) how to protect ourselves. We watched our caregivers employ boundaries that protected us. When we grow up, we become our own parents and always tap into those subconscious boundaries that we were taught. Therefore, the stable woman never jumps right in and buys the car because she instinctively knows that there is a wait time for decision making and that it takes proof in the pudding before making the buy.

Unfortunately, many of us were raised in dysfunctional settings that required us to fend for ourselves. If we were in abusive situations and our parents did not protect us, we find it more difficult as adults to choose healthy situations. We are so desperate for the "Prince" to save us that we do not have time to stop and hear the flags waving in the wind. In many cases, too, if our mothers were in denial (as in earlier generations), we have learned to continue the *good girl* syndrome and to deny the bad things that have prompted our instincts to scream at us. We were conditioned as females that, should we question anything, complain or put up a stink, then we were judged as difficult, bitchy, or other negative labels that are unbecoming. Therefore, we accept more than our male counterparts. This is why we get taken with the car mechanic, the plumber, the roofer, or anyone else who spots us for suckers.

I digress. Let us continue.

Many women are eternal optimists when it comes to trusting men. When a man looks us in the eye and speaks with sincerity, we like to believe that he is being honest. Some men, however, have master skills at story telling, lying and convincing people of things that are untrue. These are con artists or skilled manipulators. In this book, we call them *players*. We should first discuss male players in general, single or married, because there are common traits they appear to have, to which both mistresses and wives fall prey.

Players are bullshit artists who know exactly what they want before they approach you. Sadly stated, these are predators who study you carefully to determine your needs and then feed you exactly what will get you to trust them. Before you know it, you think he is such a nice guy who really cares about you; he is so interested in you that he went out of his way to remember small things you like. Watch out! It is all about his agenda. He saw you coming before you even noticed him in the far corner of the auto mall. The question we all want answered is why do these men behave in such selfish, *assholish* ways that destroy women? What makes them the way they are? During my observations, I found a common psychological profile of a player.

The painful truth defines a player as a man who meanders in and out of "relationships" with women. This *cad* comes on like a romantic savior, a real prize that adores you like you are the sun, moon, and stars all wrapped up into one. He makes you feel like you are the only woman on the planet, created just for him. You are on a *love high* and feel more special than any man has ever made you feel. The player is clever as he remembers everything you say and takes a special interest in you, and he will probably buy you cards and presents to gain your favor. He listens attentively to your darkest secrets and accepts you for who you are. This man makes sure he becomes your support network, your *everything*, and makes it a point to call you pet names with fond affection while he pursues and woos you until you think he is the dream man. He may seem like a gem in a pile of rocks but, if he appears too good to be true, he is.

Women that came from functional homes and were taught that they are special and loved sometimes find this type of man strange. They may feel smothered. Most importantly, their instincts tell them something is not right, and they are turned off to his pursuit. They are instinctively aware that nothing in this world comes without a price, much like the *You've Won the Lottery* scams that they throw out.

The woman who needs attention, however, lavishes in his pursuit. Once he has her hooked, his disposition changes like a chameleon. She suddenly notices that he does not touch her like he used to; he no longer makes her the center of his world. If I am talking to you, then you understand what I mean when I say that this man is really concerned with his own needs. This is evident when he begins to neglect you and your needs. Your heart begins to pound as you suddenly begin to see strange things happening right before your eyes that make you think he has a secret world elsewhere, and this drives you crazy. His phone is always ringing, but he refuses to answer the calls when you are around and he does not answer his phone for you at certain times. This secret world drives you crazy. To make matters worse, he has clever, viable excuses that are impossible to question, all while he seems so honest and sincere in his explanations. You feel as though you are on a schedule as he calls at the same time of the day. As time passes, he may forget to call or starts to arrive late for your date, if he does not stand you up. This is so contrary to the way he once treated you, like the only woman in the world. You obviously begin to wonder if there is another woman or if he is just not interested in you anymore. Now you have become the ardent pursuer or his affection and begin to panic, scratch and claw for his attention.

As time passes, you do not know whether or not he has another woman or if it is just that he has lost interest in you. In fact, he may have another woman, or he may be in the process of recruiting another woman before he seduces her, while you are being strung along. The player behaves in such a way because the intimacy between you is growing, and he only wants to keep you at a certain distance. He may have another girlfriend or two, or it may be that he is delving into something else that is more important to him at that moment. All you know at this point is your gut is screaming at you that something is not right.

If you are still that important to him and you put up enough commotion, he may jump through hoops again to reign you back in. He will revert back to his *Prince in pursuit* ways to gain control of you again, and he manipulates what the two of you have so that he always keeps you at the space of distance that is comfortable for him. When your anger surfaces and you confront him, he reverts back to his seductive game. You are roped back into his world again after he apologizes with puppy dog eyes and touches you with his electricity. He may give you a sob story about how things are not so good for him right now and he did not want to burden you with his problems as he promises to make things right between you.

You think he hears your concerns and will now make a concerted effort toward the relationship, but he only gets worse each time it happens. As a friend once stated, "I always thought that if he loves me and I share my deepest hurt and vulnerability with him, then he would make sure he is aware of his actions next time around, but this was not the case. It was perplexing because each time we went around in a circle he did the exact things that hurt me, but in a worse fashion. I asked him, 'Where the hell were you the last time you did this? Don't you remember how this hurt me? Why are you getting ten times worse each time?' He had no clue as to what I was talking about while he rolled his eyes like *here we go again*. His world was only about him." She was confused because an imposter kidnapped the man with whom she fell in love. No, honey, the imposter did not steal him; he was the imposter when he pursued you.

Keep in mind that players are charmers and will avoid any conflict of which they cannot charm their way out. They do not get what they want by expressing negative emotions. They are positive and charismatic men who generally do not confront anything negative and rarely do they express anger outwardly, like the car salesman we discussed earlier. They are smooth talkers that present a positive demeanor to the world, which is the very demeanor that allows them to win.

An interesting fact to understand is they are often angry men on the inside. Their rage surfaces in passive aggressive ways, which makes it harder to detect. They get even with you by doing things that make you angry, which is their means of controlling you. They manipulate through actions. It is sad because they got you in the beginning by studying you and giving you what you want and, in the end, they get rid of you by withholding what you want. They seek to bring out the negativity in you because it justifies their exit. The more of a *pain in the ass* you become, the more justification they have for dumping you because you are not "the one" after all. They got what they wanted and you fired all the shots. As one woman stated, "I would have much preferred if he shot me or screamed at me with honesty than to withhold his affection to get even with me for something I was not even aware that I did to him."

Please note that earlier in this section I added quotations

around the word relationships because these men do not have
relationships. We think of them as just that, but we can really
define them as interactions. Hard-core players do not have the
ability to have relationships with anyone. They swing from one
female branch to the next, desperately trying to get to the level
of intimacy that defines the term "relationship," but they jump
to the next branch as soon as the level of intimacy sinks (out of
the romantic fantasy stage) into the self-disclosing phase of
vulnerability. In psychological terms, it is called *commitment
phobic.*

Once you start seeing who he really is, he is off to the next,
but in a subtle way. You will begin to find out little by little that
he has a secret world to which you are not privy, and you will
expend tiresome energy making the "relationship" grow. By the
time you have invested so much, your heart will be crushed
because it never grew at all. Your "relationship" fizzled out
right under your nose. He repeatedly abandons you with one
excuse after another. You can't fight him on it if his
grandmother died or his dog got run over by a tractor or his
boss is going to write him up for another absence. He uses
elaborate, uncontestable excuses that would make you look like
a real bitch if you objected to his absence. It is a trap. The truth
is that the worse something gets in a man's life, the more he
needs the woman he loves. He would make every effort to be
with you during "sullen" times, not use them as a means to get

away from you. With that being said, who is really meeting his needs (during these times) when he tries to get away from you?

Then you are angry with yourself and feel like a fool. "Why didn't I see this coming?" Well, he did not want you to see it because he was not finished with you yet. While you were having a "relationship" with him, he was having interactions with you. Please know this is done at a subconscious level. He is not even aware that he has a problem until he hits rock bottom and even then he may remain clueless.

The player's world belongs to him, and he always keeps a section of his world secret from everyone. Think of it in these terms: He has many pillars or boxes; each pillar contains a different person with whom he has interactions. These pillars belong to him as they are a means to keep his world in control. For example, he may have a male friend he has not seen in ten years from whom he received a message on his cell phone. He makes an extra run to Home Depot to return his friend's call. This is a sneaky man. Why doesn't he make the phone call in front of his wife or in front of you? The reason is that he does not want you in his world or in his business. With cell phone in hand, he makes an excuse to go to Home Depot to buy an extra set of pliers to fix the sink faucet that does not need fixing. You do not even know about the call.

Players feel they are entitled to keep secrets, and they should not have to tell their wives, girlfriends or anyone what they do.

"You are not my mother! I don't owe you anything! Stay out of my business!" It is pompous, narcissistic arrogance, which is unacceptable when someone is in a committed relationship. Unfortunately, these men do not understand that intimacy and closeness between a man and a woman require total honesty, truth and disclosure. It requires sharing and confiding, like the best friend discussion we had at the beginning of our talk. Intimacy means one world together, not separate, sneaky worlds to which your partner is not privy. He sees this as total control, and he is the one who must have total control. If you did this, however, it would be a different story and it would be totally unacceptable to him. This is why he has yet to have a truly successful relationship, and this is why he jumps from branch to branch. Most importantly, this is why he is so isolated and lonely. People eventually figure him out and toss him by the way side. He then views himself as the victim.

The player will spend his entire life jumping from woman to woman because he has yet to trust anyone long enough to stick around after the initial romance phase of the "relationship." The older he is, the more skilled he has become and should congratulate himself on being an *A class* con artist that (most of the time) allows him to get exactly what he sets his sights on. In his defense, however, and speaking from situations I have seen, some of these players really do meet the woman of their dreams some day and become faithful to them. This may happen when he is older, after he has experienced cycles of nothingness with various women and has been humbled by abandonment. He may eventually hit rock bottom and be forced to seek professional help, probably after losing everything. Consequently, one day he may give up his fight for control and succumb to the love of a good woman.

Surprisingly enough, what these men are really afraid of is total abandonment. This man is afraid you will discover all the inadequacies that he perceives he has and then dump his ass. The player has yet to discover the honest fact that all people have inadequacies, but he cannot face the fact that he has any flaws. He needs constant adulation and appreciation. When normal issues surface, as they do in deeper levels of any "relationship," he views this as a sign that the woman will not stick around long enough to love him anyway. He may join a pity party, claiming he is not good enough for you or for any woman, which prompts you to feel sorry for him and then attempt to help him. Your codependent instincts help you act as his savior. Many times this is all an act to draw you back into his pillar, where you end up spending tiresome energy on him.

This is the trap into which most women fall. The best chance you have of changing this man is to leave him to his own destruction. People only change (if there is a chance for change) when they hit rock bottom and have to pick themselves off the ground. You cannot fix him, and you cannot reassure him that you will not abandon him. Nothing is a guarantee, especially when he sets it up to where you have to abandon him.

The player is addicted to the initial romantic, seduction phase of chasing after a woman. In fact, he may be addicted to the excitement of living on the edge, and this is true if he is a married player. He enjoys the thrill of "not" getting caught. Most importantly, the thrill (of the danger) of getting caught gives him an adrenaline rush. This is a dysfunctional man who will cause his own demise some day and, unfortunately, the demise of all the unsuspecting women who get involved with him.

As the intimacy deepens in a relationship, he will pull away and then, in many of the situations I have seen, string the poor woman along while he has his eye constantly open for other women who (he perceives) may more readily accept his shortcomings. The cycle continues. In short, the cycle of a hard-core player: he recruits you, seduces you, romances you, placates you and then discards you.

When women are entangled in this web, it makes their lives nothing but hell. It is as though they are chasing feathers in the wind, ignoring everything in their path. They lose parts of their lives. Before they know it, they lose their friends, their careers, their families, and anything else that was dear to them. All they can see is the feather in the wind, and all they know how to do is chase it, leaving everything else behind. The question remains:

Why don't they just terminate the relationships and move on?

A woman in this situation loves the man he *appeared* to be at the beginning of their "relationship." She fell in love with the imposter, and now she is forever trying to find the man with whom she fell in love. It is a lot like meeting the love of your life when he was drunk. He had a whole different persona with a great personality; he made you feel wonderful. As you get to know him, you wonder where that person went. Six months later you find out that the first two months you went on dates with him he was numb from vodka. Now that you are living with him and see him sober, you can't stand the imposter that stole your man. It is hurtful and very deceptive. This is why it is critical to get to know the man and watch the entire movie before buying the car.

Functional women do not need what he is trying to sell. In fact, they won't be sold. They do the buying on their own. The dysfunctional woman, however, becomes obsessed and determined to find the man inside the imposter. It may take several years before she hits rock bottom, faces reality, and realizes that the "imposter" was the man. She just could not face the truth that this man is not who he appeared to be. He never existed.

It is more painful to grieve without him than it is to continue forward, frantically searching for that person he appeared to be. If you constantly chase the high, you get trapped deeper below.

This is what makes the player so emotionally dangerous. If you have never been introduced to the player personality before, then it is difficult to detect the danger signs. You do not know what to watch out for. If you are an honest, lonely woman who is desperate for love, then you will be smitten by the player's charm. The danger is that a lonely woman may be swept into this man's world like being swept under an emotional tidal wave.

The unsuspecting danger is that the player, pretending to be the perfect man, ruins it for the woman when exploring future mating prospects. It is hard to be satisfied with anything else once you have had the "best." The painful truth is that no man is perfect and the good, honest guy is not going to behave in the cunning, charming, calculating manner, as are players, who make the woman tingle with joy. In fact, he may be just the opposite with an awkward, introspective personality. The woman, therefore, must retrain her mind and "settle" for less for the rest of time. This is much like the player fantasizing and masturbating to pornographic films or some other illusion. This, in turn, creates an anticlimactic situation with his wife or girlfriend because no one can compare to a "perfect" fantasy. It is dangerous territory.

The player is a dangerous man. He needs to take his interactions with women to the all-time high of fantasy love. At first, he wants you to be madly in love with him and sets it up so that you fall deep into emotional quicksand. Before you know it, you are trapped in an abyss of something that always makes you question who this man really is. In the next section we will explore the player's profile and discover what created the monster in him. It is fun if you can keep it in a box and just have fun with him, but his goal is make you fall in love with him. Sadly, most women do.

My Father's Son and My Mother's Boy

Based on my observations, I have come to see that players have unique psychological profiles. If you understand his background and unique characteristics, you will have a clearer understanding of who this man is. A real, hard-core player can be defined as a cold, empty man on the inside, but when he seduced you, had the appearance of being a compassionate, warm-hearted, giving man who understood you. At the time he expended the energy seducing you, he understood your needs. He sized you up in thirty seconds, just like a car salesman understands that you want to buy a car. It is all about him. What must he say and do to have you buy his car so he can make a profit? After you give him the money and drive away, he does not care about your sick child that has Leukemia, even though he sympathized with you for a half hour during the car negotiation phase and went into great detail about his pain over his Aunt Louise suffering from the same disease last year. He said whatever he had to say to get what he wanted. Bad boy!

But why does he behave so terribly? He does not intentionally do this. He has a psychological problem and is unconscious to the world around him. It reverts back to his childhood.

I have known many players and can safely share some similarities or common childhood traits that these men possess. Some men were raised by weak mothers who were emotionally dependent on their fathers and became abusive (to the child) when the relationship (marriage) turned sour. Some men, on the other hand, were raised by cold, domineering women who "controlled" their weak, emotionally unavailable fathers. These are the "iceberg" queens who are domineering, controlling and unfeeling. Women with such distinct traits do not have the ability to build relationships with their sons and deprive them of the ability to build intimate relationships with women. They, in turn, raise little players that will eventually destroy the lives of many women someday.

Some men were over stimulated as kids and received too much gratification at certain stages of emotional development; therefore, they get bored with everything, including women. These players constantly seek the "better" everything and are satisfied with nothing. If you are familiar with this type of man, you realize that he cannot find happiness because he is constantly searching for something or someone else. This includes women, as he continually seeks the flavor of the month. He gets bored easily and jumps from one to another, seeking the perfect mate. The pillars multiply with age. When he wakes up one morning fifty years later, he realizes the perfect woman never existed, much like the lonely woman realizes Prince Charming was only a fairytale. Both regret the wasted years chasing that which never existed. In addition, if his caretaker made him the center of attention, he was raised to believe he is the only one in the universe who matters. He seeks constant gratification without thinking of anyone else. Consequently, he eventually ends up a lonely, old man someday.

Many of the men I discuss were raised in the first category, where their weak mothers were deprived by cold fathers who were either absent, abusive, emotionless and/or a combination of all three. Let us say, for example, that the player's mother was exceptionally weak and had little respect for herself in the relationship with her husband. In essence, she was submissive to his father, much like Edith Bunker doing a marathon run for Archie's beer, right after he calls her a Ding Bat (sitcom, *All in the Family*, 1971). Let us continue. The Ding Bat then kisses him on the forehead, "Oh, Archie, how was your day? Dinner is on the table...come and sit and we'll have a nice stew I made today!" Now take it one more step further. Archie then raises his hands: "Edith, I don't have time for that now! Stretch Cunningham is coming over to talk shop about old man Hanson! Put it away, Edith!" He then groans as he pushes the stew away that she slaved over all day just for him. The Ding

Bat then smiles at him in obedient submission. She refuses to hold this man accountable, allowing him to treat her with little regard.

The player learns at a very early age that he can neither respect his mother, nor can he trust her to tend to his needs. She was more preoccupied by the beer and stew to please his father, no matter if the man was a cold-hearted *son of a bitch*. Unfortunately, the child learned that a man has the power to control a woman emotionally. The deprived woman may then fly off the handle with her son because she is neglected by his father. The obsession over her husband makes her reactive and unstable. After time passes, she may become nice to the child out of guilt (for her own inadequacies). It is no wonder the boy is confused about his feelings for his mother. He ends up having a love-hate relationship with her. Unfortunately, he realizes he cannot trust her and has little respect for the weak woman she is. He carries this "baggage" with him to all his future relationships. He obviously experienced great trauma at some stage of development, which may have stunted his emotional growth.

The player also learns at a very early age that he is a male, just like his father, and desperately tries to gain approval and acceptance from him. All he gets in return is surface interactions, like how to take the trash out or how to fix something. This is not the Ward Clever dad that sits down with

Wally struggling with a heart-felt discussion over Wally's feelings, but rather a very controlled, cold environment that teaches this boy to have only surface interactions that meet a specific purpose at the time (sitcom, *Leave it to Beaver*, 1957). Wally Clever learns that he is not only a human being, but he is a boy who is entitled to feelings. The player learns that he is a *Meat Head* (sitcom, *All in the Family*, 1971), should he try to discuss feelings.

When the player grows into manhood, he has very little respect for women, and he is fearful of men. He may appear to have male friends, but his real friends are other women. This man relates better to women because he can overpower them and, since his self-esteem is very low, he has very few meaningful relationships with men. To say the least, the player is an empty, cold man who is very lonely on the inside. If he can neither trust nor respect women, and he can't relate to other men, who is left? We can extrapolate from this that he builds a fortress around his inner core and grabs at anything to fill him up.

Many players are dreamers who jump from one job to the next or from one fantasy to the next. Many dream of being wrapped in a thick film of apotheosis with God-like qualities that everyone worships. They may strive to be the greatest actor, artist, musician, or any other professional that will give them fame, power or glory. They have a driven need to feed their egos — to be glorified, loved and worshiped. They need constant stroking that can be all-consuming and annoying after a while. If he doesn't get it, he gets bored and moves onto the next. Realistically speaking, no woman can meet his needs.

Further, should you become suspicious and question them about anything, they can intellectualize and manipulate you into believing you are insane. This is commonly known as *crazy making*. If you are involved with a man like this, you know I am right. It becomes your insanity that prompted you to question why his sweater smelled of perfume. He will do whatever he has to keep you under this thumb. Take a look at this reaction to poor Alice who sees all the signs her husband is playing around on her: "Here we go again, Alice! I get home from a hard day's work to make money for you and you accuse me again of this shit! It was old lady Gloria who hugged me goodbye today. You remember my sixty year-old secretary, Alice? I guess I am screwing her too, huh?" He slams the door and bursts into the garage to escape his wife's relentless attack. Poor Alice is left feeling shamed, stupid, ridiculed, attacked, and *crazy*. She is consumed with guilt for causing problems for her "poor" husband who is doing so much for her. She dismisses the fact that his suit jacket reeks of women's cologne and has lipstick on the collar. By this time, she is such an emotional wreck that she goes overboard trying to make it up to him with apologies, much like Edith Bunker apologizing for making

Archie a stew on the day Stretch Cunningham was arriving. What Alice does not understand is that confronting him does not work. Had Alice said nothing, packed her bags, and threw his jacket at him while walking out the door, she would have made her case without being dehumanized by his narcissistic arrogance. A word of caution: The player always wins, Ladies. You cannot pin him down; you cannot change him; you can't get to the bottom of anything. His onerous mind is always three steps ahead: plotting, planning, organizing and scheming. You are the loser.

Deep in the mind of the player is the desire for total control of everything and everyone, for deep in his inner core lives the desperate fear of having control over nothing.

My Prince, Defined

When you look at your current situation with your man, try not to turn a blind eye to anything that makes you question him. You may be one of the lucky ones who found an otherwise honest man who has been faithful to his wife all this years until you came along. He may be miserably unhappy with his wife, and you might be the dream girl he waited for his whole life. Most women prefer to have this type of married lover rather than the hard-core, predatory player who has a wife and several girlfriends, all of whom believe they are the only ones. Then again, you could be dealing with a hard-core player who finally found you after fifty-something years and seeks no longer. This man may see no way out of his marriage, but his heart belongs to you. If you are honest with yourself, you know the answer right now. If he took his time getting involved with you in the beginning of your relationship and battled with is conscience before caving into his feelings for you, then you might not be dealing with a married player. If he was awkward and unpolished in his pursuit of you, then you may not be dealing with a player. He might just be a man in an unhappy marriage that is unwilling to tell the truth to his wife. Again, the choice is yours.

Please Show Me A Faithful Prince

With all this talk about unfaithful men, it is discouraging enough to throw up our hands and forget them all together. Do not be discouraged. Remember, we are weeding out the good from the bad. This entire book is devoted to the signs of our unfaithful counterparts; therefore, we are focusing on them. Faithful men do exist. Before we begin our girl-to-girl discussion here about the faithful man, we must have a heart-to-heart talk about men in general.

Men are polygamists by nature. Face it, guys look at women. They are wired this way, and a wise, secure woman understands this. This is why super bowl commercials with beautiful women always make the most profit. This is why the Playboy industry has made millions from magazines showing beautiful naked girls. This is why the Christian movement is forever fighting the porno industry because the main audience is men. The fact is men are driven by testosterone. The primary "male" function in our *cave man ancestry* days was to generate as much sperm as possible to impregnate females and reproduce so that our species would not go extinct. It worked because we still exist and are procreating more than ever; we just need to learn to cohabitate a little better.

Even though men look at women, it means very little to the faithful man. It is true that men tend to be polygamists by nature, but many functional men prefer monogamous relationships with good women. Many men understand the value of fidelity and long for the same family unit as women. Some men know that when they see a beautiful woman in a bank, for instance, that they are just admiring beauty and then return to their wives. The beauty in the moment stays behind in the moment. They understand that moments pass, but their actions forever remain. He does not fantasize for hours about the woman in the bank, nor does he masturbate at the thought of her. If you ask, he may say, "I simply think it is wrong to cheat around!" End of story! Women who are secure within themselves understand this and are not threatened by this.

The question still remains: What causes some men to be faithful and others to be unfaithful? Part of it is cultural traditions, racial and socioeconomic values, and some of it is just plain DNA. Those stinking genes! A large defining factor, however, is how they were raised.

I would like to make a special point to briefly discuss culture. This book is designed for those living in traditional cultures. If we look at the Middle East, for example, surely the information in this book need not apply because the political and social structures are the antithesis of American society. It is unfortunate that women are viewed as property or objects, contrary to equal partners. Other cultures, too, have conflicting views of marital fidelity and equality. In some cultures it is expected that a man will have a wife and women on the side. It depends on cultural mores and what is expected and allowed.

I would also like to note that our society has been advancing and growing in our topic of conversation. Both men and women are becoming enlightened, contrary to couples fifty years ago. It is important to note that there are fewer "faithful" men because there have been far too many betrayed (needy and insecure) women in history who have unknowingly (unintentionally) raised and groomed little players. The generational cycle continues.

Although *Leave it to Beaver* is as much of a fairytale as *Cinderella,* there is some truth to fiction here. Had *Leave it to Beaver* been a real life family, Wally and Beaver Clever would have made loving, faithful husbands. It was the quality in the *relationship-building* skills they learned that would have made them great "catches" for the ladies. A man who was raised in an accepting environment, like Wally and Beaver, have an inner sense of contentment and are not constantly on the prowl for something else. They escape the perpetual longing and yearning that unfaithful men possesses, that which drives them to chase women and crave more and more of whatever it is that they can't get enough of.

Faithful men understand that relationships are much deeper than the initial romantic phase of attraction. They take the good with the bad and are accepting of their weaknesses, as well as those of their partners. They have fewer expectations and less criticism, both of which cause unfaithful men to keep moving on to the next woman. For example, a faithful man does not need adulation and flirtations from dozens of women to feel like "more" of a man, nor does he need constant praise. He already knows he is a man because his mother assured him years earlier that he is lovable, even when he failed, much like June Clever's relationships with her boys.

Faithful men are reared by strong, decisive mothers who are nurturing and loving; they set firm limits and boundaries with their sons These mothers are not ruled and guided by their husbands' responses to them or lack thereof; their sons learn that they are safe with them. They learn that they can trust their mothers to follow through, protect them and teach them right from wrong without persecution. These women teach their sons how to be men of worth and build their confidence. For example, good mothers will thank their small sons for trying to fix the same thing Daddy fixed yesterday. Mom understands he is imitating his father and shows him appreciation for his attempts. She is stable and consistent in her commitment to her sons, no matter what is happening in the relationship with her husband. The boy feels proud and confident as his self worth continues to grow into a well- adjusted man someday who is capable of loving. When he matures into manhood, he does not jump from one female tree to the next, like the Player, trying to escape his inadequacies.

Faithful men are also reared by strong, masculine fathers who teach them how to be men. If his father was a faithful man, then he has a better chance of being faithful. Ward Clever, for example, taught his sons to be responsible and reliable. He showed them how to be men of honesty and sincerity. Confident men, like Mr. Clever, are not afraid to talk to their sons about issues that could be considered "matters of the heart." Reared in this type of environment, boys are taught that it is okay to talk about things, and they need not worry about Daddy yelling, "Don't cry like a sissy girl!" These fathers are not abusers, nor are they emotional avoiders. They encourage their sons and teach them how to make sound judgments without using the belt to correct undesired behaviors. Therefore, their needs were met during the maturation process.

Both parents play important roles in the types of mates these men become. If you want to use this information to help you figure out your situation, you may want to consider a few points. If he had a wonderful father who was dependable, reliable and available, then he will most likely be a "better" man. You can sum a man up very quickly by the relationship he has with his mother and by the way he describes her. Most importantly, the way he treats his mother will tell you everything you need to know about him. You know you have a keeper if his father genuinely loved his mother.

The Courtyard of an
Unfaithful Prince

Oh, Noble Man, Prince of the Land, I give to
you my all, as I am a servant to you.

6

Positioning for Prey

In the competitive times in which we now live, it can seem impossible to find single, available men that are from "faithful" stock. Lonely women in their thirties often fall prey to handsome men in powerful positions because they love attention from men who have clout. Unfortunately, many women have been single for such a long period of time that they have become desperate. All of the sudden Mr. Boss comes along and sweeps them off their feet. This is a terrible situation in which a woman can put herself. Even if he is married, his attention is flattering and somewhat comforting, but this mistake can lead her to the unemployment line. Married players in powerful positions like to play, but they do not like to pay the price.

The Undertow

Most of us have been to the ocean during the summertime when the waves are healthy and furious. If you wander too far off shore, you risk being sucked in the undertow current that moves you out to sea because the undertow pulls the water from shore. If you get caught in this undertow, you are in serious trouble. You are swept from underneath and before you know it, you are drowning. This is synonymous to what happens many times when we get involved with married players in high positions that like to chase women. Before you know it, you are sucked into a mistress prison and will spend countless days and nights trying to figure out how you got into this mess but, most importantly, how to get out?

If I am talking to you, then you can identify with what I am saying. You know he is married, but you tell yourself that you really don't want him anyway if he is acting unfaithful to someone else. At this point it is fun. You do not feel guilty because he tells you his other half is a terrible wife and a horrible mother, which justifies his infidelity. Perhaps you may be a better woman (to him) than his wife and continue to enjoy his advances. At this point, you are not invested because he is just a friend who needs someone to talk to. All of the sudden, you find yourself attracted to him and, before you know it, you are jumping in the sack with him and cannot wait to take your next breath until he is with you again.

As you grow closer together, he continues to make you feel like the only woman on the planet. You are becoming quit possessive of him and no longer want to be "just" the friend. You now want to be the chosen woman. It is also a compliment to you that he wants you, not his wife, or at least that is what he tells you. His romantic words of *fantasy tomorrows* capture your emotional identity in the moment.

Some women become cemented in his romantic words and stay for years in this stage of the affair. What next? Years pass and you are still cemented in this romantic stage. He is getting everything he wants from you, but you still do not have what his wife has. You are living in his fantasy while your "pretty" years are passing you by. There is no chance of a monogamous relationship because of his other obligations, but this is what you are willing to accept. Many women do not see that this situation may eventually destroy their lives.

Aphrodisiac

The sad point I must stress is that there are so many married players that are smooth operators, very skilled, because they have had much experience recruiting women. In most cases, they find their women in the workplace because, realistically, they spend the majority of their time on the job. If you know someone who has gotten involved with a man such as this, then you surely understand the dangers involved. When he glances at a cute little secretary with a short skirt, high heels and a delightful figure, his head in his pants starts to swell. The temptation is overwhelming. Contrary to what many believe, I contend it is not the position that makes the guy a player, but it is the guy who seeks the powerful position to continue playing.

This is tied into the player personality traits. If he loves women, then he will find them no matter what he does. If he craves a powerful position, he is sure to attract women like bees to honey: rock stars, administrators, actors, politicians, doctors, lawyers, etc.

The reason so many players can advance their games with women is that there are far too many available women ready to play their games. If women refused to be pawns for these men, they would have no one to play with. However, if a man in a powerful position takes an interest in his subordinate at work, it may be difficult for her to resist. Power is an aphrodisiac and symbolizes strength, and women love strong, powerful men. The player knows this all too well and uses it to his advantage. The "groupie" women that flock to rock bands, for example, can make fools of themselves. If you throw yourself at a womanizer, he will be more than happy to use you. Aren't you worth much more than this?

Every woman wants to be special and the "chosen woman," and a powerful man has the ability to turn on many women. Again, it all reverts back to what we want in the long run. If you want to play and are not looking for anything else, then you have less of a chance of being hurt. Most women, however, function in denial while they tell themselves they do not want anything more than what he is giving, but then become filled with resentment when the affair does not go anywhere. This can be very dangerous, especially if the situation culminated in the workplace and has a direct affect on her job. I must mention how dangerous it is for women to become romantically involved with their supervisors. Married players in powerful positions often use their positions to seduce naïve women and then dump them when they have either tired of them or become threatened when they get too attached. In the end, she loses.

I once knew an older woman in the medical field who made a profound statement that has always remained with me: "I used to attend meetings where all the physicians gathered. It made me sick to my stomach to see these high ranking, married guys *use* these young interns. These women were seduced by the aphrodisiac of power. They'd play with them like they were toys and then discard them." These women were clueless because players can be smooth-talking, fast operating seductive charmers. They did not know how to tell the difference between sex and love, and these guys were using them for a good roll in the hay. This is an undertow that can ruin their careers.

An honorable man, however, will not behave so badly. No matter what naked woman may stand before him, he will not stray. He will not succumb to such unacceptable transgressions because it is not a part of his "noble" DNA. He has enough self discipline to avoid falling from Grace. He realizes that there is always a tomorrow when he will have to answer for today. These men are rare, but they do exist.

First, it is important to note that no matter how good a liar you are and no matter how good you are at covering things up, there is always someone somewhere who knows what you are doing. You can never truly compartmentalize your feelings because sexual attraction and love cannot be captured in a pillar. If you are having a fling at work, people will eventually *pick up* on your secret affair by reading your body language and romantic energy, which can be spotted a mile away. Once the gossip begins and your career flushes down the toilet, it is next to impossible to put the Jeannie back in the bottle. It is difficult to repair a damaged reputation.

Most affairs are exposed by those involved in the affair, especially the women. It is the unintended consequences of telling someone a secret. Always remember that there is no such thing as *I am going to tell you something, but you can't tell anyone.* It does not work this way. Once a piece of information gets out, it floats like a runaway orb and you can't retrieve it. You can't contain it either. Once the gossip mill heats up and the stress mounts, most women cannot take the heat and need someone to lean on for support. Consequently, they make the mistake of telling one coworker and, low and behold, the orb is out of their control.

It may be true that we all want to be that one special woman, especially to a man who is *way up there* in charge of everyone else. What a special honor to be "his." I am here to tell you that being "his" can land you on the unemployment line. If push comes to shove, he will push you under the bus. If you become a threat to him when people gossip or when someone goes to his wife, you are the *mistress no more*. Your reputation may be jeopardized because you will become the *home wrecker*, the *easy one*, the *bitch*, the *whore*, because society, as we discussed, does not condone (what is perceived as) your behavior. I have seen it happen. You are the expendable one.

The first thing married players do when they are busted is apologize to their wives and children. Rarely, if ever, are there any acknowledgements to the women they actively seduced and used. The one exception was Mark Sanford, the Congressman from South Carolina, who came forward publically to announce his love for his "soul mate," as he proclaimed. At least this man came forward (at the demise of his career) with the truth instead of spinning more lies. No matter what we think of him, we can at least give him a gold star for confessing and stopping the lies. Most players in high position act in dastardly ways that are a true embarrassment to the male race. Think about the numerous politicians that cannot keep their peckers in their pants. The first thing they do, again, is apologize to their wives. It is as though they borrow speeches from each other in their *little black books of adultery*. If it weren't so destructive and hurtful, it would be comical. We can continue on with various names of celebrities and the like, but it would be the same results: apologize to the wife and kids while dumping the mistress under the bus. The bottom line is that these men are destructive, dishonest and highly flammable individuals. They may have money, fame and power, but they are desperately poor in honor. Again, it all reverts back to the character and upbringing. A self-disciplined man who has honor does not allow power to go to his head, and I am not talking about the head above his neck.

Compartmentalized Love

Before we proceed any further, we must define what the word *love* means to a married player. They can use the term like it is disposable. I think a more realistic term for his love is *compartmentalize*. If you are dating a married player, this chapter is definitely for you, and you will most likely identify with the message. Let us analyze what you are to him and what every other person in his life means to him, especially his wife.

First, think back to the pillars I was referring to earlier. Each person in his life is in a separate pillar or box. He jumps in and out of each pillar when he chooses to have interactions with the person(s) in a specific pillar at the time. Rarely do the pillars meet. Each time he goes into that pillar, that person becomes the most important person to him at that moment.

Let us digress for a moment so that we fully grasp this concept. We all compartmentalize at one time or another. We love our mothers, fathers, and siblings. We love our dear friends and our children. We express our love for them in a variety of ways. In a sense, we compartmentalize these people and put them into boxes, pillars, or categories. When we are with them during the holidays, for example, we focus on them and forget our day-to-day lives. When the festivities pass, we forget them as we revert back to our daily routines.

When it comes to intimate relationships, however, we tend to sink deeper in the seed of intimacy and have more meaningful "relationships" than just holiday interactions. We are vulnerable in every sense of the word. This is what your man vowed to do when he stood at the alter putting a ring on his wife's finger. This *deeper* love is much different than the other loves he has in his life because it is a contractual partnership in the eyes of the law. It is disclosing everything to the other half to whom he made the life-long commitment. The problem is that a player can't relinquish control or trust anyone with his deepest secrets. He sections off places to put people, places that do not intrude on his comfort zone. He never fully opens to this commitment and continues to maintain his pillars, as he did when he was single. In fact, he may keep his old pillars while building new ones with different people. He is a sneaky man who destroys any relationship before it starts.

Shall we digress to insert a brief point about equivocation? The player is absolutely clueless to the fact that when he equivocates, or lies, he fractures any intimacy he hopes to build in his "relationships." This is detrimental to his long-term, emotional well-being. He does not realize that nothing kills a relationship or the potential for any relationship more that dishonesty — even one lie cracks the bond. One lie added to another lie, which is added to another lie creates a huge wall of distrust. If it is not the distrust that first kills it, it is the guilt he subconsciously harbors that forces him to distance from his partner.

Let us return to our original scenario.

The moment he takes a vow to his wife, he begins a life with her. He married her because he wanted to build a life with her. He loved her so much that, in most cases, he even had children with her. Then responsibility and reality set in. The pressures began to mount, as they often do in marriage, and he began to stray like a cat in heat. He longed to escape from the reality of what is expected of him because he could not stand the demands on him. Then you came into his life and brought him comfort, relief and excitement. As with any relationship, the initial phase is romantic infatuation where you both are on your best behaviors and succumb to the feeling of total acceptance. At this point, there are no expectations because the relationship has not been built yet. You are the "fun." You are his fantasy-high while he deprives the woman he married.

After enough time passes, he has you on the side, but his wife has the house, the fancy car and all the other perks that come with *wife* status. She has her name on his bank account and together they are one in the eyes of the law. They probably have children together, which is a bond for life between them. What do you have with him that indicates that his words of love are anything other than the same types of love he has for those other people in his life with whom he does not share physical intimacy, such as his mother, father, siblings, or children? Yet, he will hold your face, look you in the eye and tell you he is in love with you, all while unzipping your pants with a solid penis ready to explode. When you have your love making session, he lies next to you and thanks you so much for being in his life because you are so special to him. He does not know what he would do without you. In fact, he cannot live without you. You keep him sane and take him away from that "crazy" woman in his home, as he would have you perceive. However, what he is really running from is responsibility. Jumping into a pillar with you gives him *mojo* to go back to his responsibility and commitments. It is comparable to recharging a battery. Where does this leave you? What exactly is his love for you? Most importantly, who recharges your battery?

Love is supposed to be a way of life, at least in the context he is using it. He is speaking to you like he is ready to take you to the altar, but no action follows. Should you talk about a future together, he conveniently changes the subject or deflects the conversation. If you watch his body language, you will see him squirm when the topic surfaces. After all, he says he cannot live without you, but this man takes no action at all to do anything other than speak words of love to you and then walk out your door. Again, if this is a convenient situation for you and this is all that you want, then you will not be as hurt. Most women, however, find it difficult to dangle at the end of his string. Resentment mounts and then eventually something breaks, explodes, implodes or forces a choice to be made, if I may use passive voice for emphasis.

If you are in love with this man and want him to leave his wife for you, you may have a problem because he has compartmentalized you to the point of total confusion. Your life may be stopped because it is hard to focus on other things when you are living in one world with him while he has (probably) compartmentalized you. You are his fantasy while he is your reality. Most likely you will drown in an abyss of questions, and it will be difficult for you to get to the bottom of anything. He will avoid your seriousness and keep you in a web of charming words. You may become, as many women do, resentful and start to feel used like a toy. Eventually, you will come to a fork in the road that will force you to change course.

Not a Through Street

When you come to a fork in the road, you have to change direction. When the road ends and you are prohibited from going straight, you must take an alternate route. This is so true

in dead-end relationships that have *Not a Through Street*
vibrations. Let us answer some question that expand on this
point. A married man may take you to dinner and may buy you
presents, but where is he Christmas Eve? Where is he Christmas
Day? Where is he on the weekends and every night of the week
when you are in a lonely, cold bed? To whom does he give his
true commitment? Where is he when you have to be driven to
the doctor because you have a 102 temperature and cannot drive
a vehicle? I bet he is with his wife and kids and "can't get
away." Yet, he will meander back to you Monday with an email
or phone call telling you how much he missed you and
desperately needs to see you this week. "How about
Wednesday?" This gives him a day in advance to set his wife
up for his absence in two days from now. Is this fair to you? If
you do not want him as a mate and are using him as he is using
you, then you will not be as devastated as most would be in this
type of situation.

In closing this section, I call a married man's love,
compartmentalized love because his love for you is in a closed
pillar. He jumps in and out of it when he feels the need to be
with you. When you are not a priority, he is out of the pillar
doing whatever else he wants. He owes nothing to you. He
keeps a tight lid (on you) in this box while he lives his life and
takes care of everyone else: his wife, kids, in-laws, friends,
family members, work relations, and anything else. You are left

alone in the dark while he lives his life with his wife. Again, this is a choice a woman makes, and it is a wise woman that decides what she wants before becoming entangled in webs that destroys her life. It is also a wise woman that listens to what a man does and pays very little attention to what he says. I believe people do what they want to do, and there is no such thing as, "I cannot leave my wife because of the kids." In fact, the kids are the least of his worries. It is the wife, honey. He probably feels so guilty (if he is capable of feeling guilt) that he can't stand it. Chances are probable that she is not the terrible apostle of abuse he had you believe, which is almost impossible for a mistress to assimilate.

One point to note is that the married player lives his life in neutral. Rarely does he take action in any area of his life and, in the most cases, he may never leave his wife, even when he gets busted. In fact, if his wife leaves him, he may beg her forgiveness and do whatever he can to win her back. For a while, that is. Although he may desperately want a divorce, the thought of ending it is too terrifying for him to handle. He cannot stand abandonment and the thought of ending anything makes him panic as much as the thought of beginning something does. Even if he wants a divorce and his wife asks if there is another woman, he may repudiate with fear and demand she not talk that way. Again, he is terrified of taking any action. This point is exemplified in the movie *Walk the Line* (the story of Johnny Cash), when his wife hauled out of the driveway. He really loved June Carter and wanted to be with her, but he took no action to be with her. When his wife finally had enough and was leaving with the kids, he was still directing her to return. This type of emotional paralysis destroys lives. He could not stand the ending, as endings, again, are painful. Players, given their common profile and childhood experiences, avoid pain at all costs and avoid taking any action that forces the hand of change.

After a woman has been involved with a married man for a while, she begins to see his deficits and flaws, but she may not understand them. She may begin to take things personally and, perhaps, put pressure on him to leave his wife. Perhaps she may give him an ultimatum that he, nine times out of ten, does not have the courage to follow through. He may attempt to gain sympathy from her by telling her he would be a terrible father if he left his "poor" kids and his wife who has been so patient with him after all these years. "She is the mother of my kids. I can't do that to her." Many married men hide behind their kids by telling naive mistresses (who they convince) *how hard it would be* to leave them. The truth of the matter is that he is afraid to leave, and his wife may be his security blanket or anchor that keeps him stable. He does not realize that "security" is not love and, if you are his true love, he is being unfair to you by trapping you in his pillar. Again, it is your choice.

Compartmentalized love is very hard for mistresses to understand, identify and accept because it has to do with a lifestyle and a certain way of thinking. Compartmentalized love is indicative of men who are incapable of having relationships. They can only maintain interactions, and everything is what they want at the moment. Those who have the ability to cultivate relationships can't grasp this idea of *fragmented pieces* of relationships. I once knew a therapist who said that compartmentalizing is worrisome because those that are on the receiving end of his compartmentalizing have a difficult time determining what his truth really is. There is a lack of sincerity and true commitment to anyone and anything in his life. Again, he keeps everyone in a pillar, prompting them to believe what he wants them to believe. If you are on the receiving end or you are trapped in one of his pillars, your needs are certainly not being met.

If you are involved with a married player, he may truly feel tremendous love and devotion for you while he is with you, and he may love you more than any other woman in his life, but he leaves it right there for the next time he comes back. It is difficult to even comprehend unless you think the way he does. It is difficult to understand, especially when you are so in love with him and want him to treat you out of the bedroom as he does in the bedroom when your clothes are off. What started as fun has now turned into pain and rejection because you realize he is not choosing you. You are not the chosen woman after all. Many women relive the same childhood pain of abandonment over and over again, and this married player is the catalyst that forces them to do just that.

Princess Plural

Up until now I have written this book as though the married player has a wife and one woman on the side. In many cases there are numerous women who are waiting in the wings that have no idea there are several other women. No matter how we feel about this or what perceptions are attached to this type of behavior, it does happen more often than we would like to think. Rather than have him lynched, it is much more productive and enlightening to accept that there are men like this and stay far away from them. If I am talking to you, the player, there is a chapter coming up that will help, should you commit to change your ways.

The man who is married with several women on the side has all the attributes of the predatory, serial player with additional characteristics to his personality. This man is an insecure woman's worst nightmare. In order to weave several lives into separate pillars and deceive women to this degree, there must be a serious character deficit that drives a man to hurt women the way he does. The only difference between this man and the serial rapist is that one inflicts physical harm, which can be seen. A serial player inflicts wounds, scars and bruises on women that are invisible to the naked eye. When a woman gives her heart to a man and he plays her for a "fool," it can have devastating consequences. Further, if a man has such little regard that he has several women on a string, he must harbor a great deal of anger and resentment toward women, much as the serial rapist does. Keep in mind that rape is not about sex, and it certainly is not about intimacy. It is about rage. Somewhere in this man's past, he probably had serious emotional wounds inflicted on him and now takes it out on as many women as he can.

If it was not his mother, then it may have been another female caretaker who scarred his self esteem; consequently, he spent his life (subconsciously) hurting them. This man needs several women that he can manipulate and play with like putty in his hands, like a chess game that he makes sure he wins. In addition, this man may suffer from severe commitment phobia and may have several addictions: gambling, drinking, sex, pornography, drugs, or some other compulsion that is way beyond his control. Whatever the case, he has a serious psychological problem and would benefit from professional help. It would be wise for him to explore the reasons for his lack of ability to give and receive intimacy. Moreover, it would be wise for him to explore the depth of his anger and personal insecurities that drive him to deceive the way he does.

It is devastating to the women who are involved with him because it is comparable to being ripped off and "taken for a ride," much like he slowly depleted the money in your bank account all while watching you frantically search for the lost funds. This type of betrayal is downright cruel and dangerous. Unfortunately, women tend to take it personally and blame themselves for his deceptive behavior. They may feel unworthy or unlovable and may believe he sought other women because of their own inadequacies, just as it is typical that the victim in a rape case may blame herself. The cruel reality is that this is his problem and his problem alone. He sought other women because of his own dysfunction, and he would have behaved this way no matter who he was with because he cannot sustain an intimate relationship with anyone.

Statistics have shown that very rarely can a severe commitment phobic recover. First, he has to want to get help and needs to have the courage to explore the reasons for his problems. He has to realize he has a problem and take responsibility for his actions. If he apologizes and makes false admissions to his perceived problem, then it may be a direct ploy to manipulate you so that you take him back again.

The real work in these situations is done by the wife and mistresses because everyone has to pick themselves off the floor and try to rebuild their lives. The hardest part for these women is rejecting his advances and pleas for another chance because they don't want to believe that repeat offenders tend to repeat the same behaviors. Again, it reverts back to finding the courage to accept total reality. Will he change? Can he change? Is the hurt too deep that change cannot overcome the damage? Again, ask yourself what you want in the long run.

Wanted: The Perfect Mistress

Oh, Fair Maiden, please don't weep. I shall
return one day to you for keeps.

7

A Maiden with No Prince

Players and womanizers are skilled at zooming in on single women without husbands or boyfriends with whom they must compete. They want mistresses who will be faithful, committed, and devoted to them without demands or expectations in return. They get enough of that at home from their wives. They usually prey upon reserved women who are sensitive, loyal and nurturing and may be of "lesser status," like rescuing the damsel in distress. He loves power and control, which does not come without a price. Consequently, many women end up like Repunzel in the tower and are unaware that they are trapped until they cannot escape, especially if he is your supervisor at work or a financial resource, as we will discuss later.

The perfect mistress for a married player is someone he can trust completely and someone who will always be there for him. He is in control and when he is ready to see her, she should be grateful that he went out of his way to see her. Mistresses have no entitlement to anything, yet he wants all the perks from her.

It is a sad fact that women delude themselves sometimes into his fantasy world, believing they are everything in the world to him when he has scheduled them in and abandon them again and again.

Yes, there does appear to be a double standard. While he is at home fornicating with his wife on Saturday nights, he assumes you are home alone in your bed dreaming of him. If he senses you might be with someone else, he may begin to pull away because he fears abandonment. He may become insanely jealous, but not enough to divorce his wife and marry you because he is incapable of taking action. It does not matter (to him) that you are lonely and may want a husband to meet your needs. His needs matter, and your needs are irrelevant.

Many women make the mistake of trying to make their married players jealous by suggesting prospects of other men. Not only is this a dishonest, manipulative ploy but, depending on this situation, it may be a complete waste of energy. The outcome is almost always the same. He may act insanely jealous and may even hire someone to spy on her, as did Bugsy Siegel with Virginia Hill, but he never did leave his wife. His wife ended up leaving him, as did Johnny Cash's wife, all while begging (the wife he did not love) to stay with him.

In other cases, the mistress's jealous ploy backfires. Instead of jealousy prompting him to divorce his wife and commit to you before you get away, he may begin to think he cannot trust you. He knows you want a "real" relationship with a husband and, eventually, you will leave him anyway because he has no intention of divorcing his wife. Although he may pursue you more in a selfish effort to make sure he still has you under his thumb, he will revert back to his wife for faithfulness. You will be shoved into the very back pillar of his life for good.

The Other Prince's Wife

I have seen situations where married men partner with married women, which is an affair on equal ground because they are both playing around on their spouses. It is important to note that the married player will more outwardly use this type of woman and will have less respect for her because she is being unfaithful to her husband (with him). As irritating as this may sound, this is who he is. It remains a double standard, but this is the way he thinks. Remember that he is the center of his universe. He has calculated immediately that he cannot trust her, so he will not invest much in her. She becomes a *sometimes fuck*, as callous as it may sound. Although she is doing exactly what he is doing and has done, he may look down upon her. He much prefers his faithful, single maiden to wait upon him. Crudely stated, he likes to know that no other dick is getting inside his possession

The Interior of his
Unfaithful Kingdom

I will love you with all my heart, all my soul, and with every breath I take. That is until I hath return to my wife.

8

The Decorated Kingdom

Thus far we have discussed the life of the mistress and the wife, but now let us talk about life inside his world. He is webbing lives of deception, two of which we know for sure but, given he keeps compartmentalized pillars, there could be more. He has to please his supervisor at work, his wife, the kids, and you, all while orchestrating his world on a time schedule because everything has to be planned in advance. At first, it is his fantasy come true because he has a secret world with you that no one knows about, which is exciting for him. He looks forward to being with you once or twice a week because you take him away from the obligations of his kids and *pain in the ass* wife, as he would tell you, but then something happens.

As the "relationship" or interactions between you deepen, he has to become more skilled in his planning. After a while, his wife becomes suspicious of all those Thursday night rotary meetings and the one hour store runs to pick up bread that would normally take him five minutes. Pretty soon, his wife is cancelling his Thursday rotary meetings and is glued to him while he is in the computer room. Before you know it, he has canceled on you last Thursday and is not sending you as many emails. The plans you made together are either canceled or rescheduled. This frustrates you. You notice he disappears often, and you feel like a fool because now he is treating you as he treats his wife. The pressure begins to mount. You do not think it is his wife who is taking his attention because he tells you that they have no relationship and he cannot stand her. As far as you know, he has nothing to do with her. She is an object in the home that is of no importance to him. So who could it be? Is it another woman? Something is not right.

His wife is no object. In fact, she is probably very demanding and controlling because this is the type of woman a player chooses for a wife. Chances are she is very much in love with him. The chances are very probable, too, that he loves both you and his wife, but harbors a great deal of subconscious guilt that he may not be able to feel. His behaviors become erratic and his emotional connections to both you and his wife become schizophrenic-like. He is on a hot-and-cold cycle that clearly signifies he is "connecting" somewhere else. His wife also notices, only she does not know who it is, and you think it is someone else besides his wife. He produces a world of suspicion.

The player does not take responsibility for the pain he

creates and may sink into a rut of self pity. He has a deep-rooted fear of abandonment and cannot stand to think of his wife leaving him, but he would never tell you this. At the same time, he (sometimes) can't stand being married to her and will do whatever necessary to avoid this feeling, all while telling you he loathes her. This man begins to accept the fact that he made a poor decision years ago by marrying his wife, but now tells himself that he must accept the choices he made. Money is also a strong consideration as he fears his wife will take him to the cleaners, especially if he makes good money.

In many cases this is true. Most men are not celebrities and will not make another twenty million dollars on another movie that will supplement the amount he has to pay in a divorce settlement. He does not want to be saddled with child support and alimony. He also fears his kids will resent him for leaving the family. He perseverates on what others will think of him if he leaves his wife and kids because, to the player, image means everything. He is certain society will look down upon him and, if he is a religious man, may fear going to hell or some other dreadful place to repent for his sins. Consequently, he continues to live the *status quo* life that is comfortably numb in the world of no action whatsoever. And then someday he will wonder why he has to take the needle out of his son's arm for the fifth time down in the gutter of town, and he may hit the roof when his daughter is "being used" (as he tells her) by a married man for the second time (one would never guess why he would assume this), and he may be pissed off at the thought of bailing his youngest child out of jail for the sixth time — all while blaming the numerous mistresses he had in the past, and never once taking a good, long look at the wife with whom he was never in love, but refused to leave. And all for the sake of the children.

The player may eventually break it off with you and promise himself that he will be faithful to his wife, which may last about a week or until he can no longer stand it. He may then return to you, which makes his wife suspicious again. She may now cancel the Monday night meetings because she tightens the chains when he has gotten too far away from her. Now he must think of another meeting on Tuesday nights and generate proof to his wife that it is legitimate so she will "get off his ass," as he thinks. His life is anything but peaceful and, if he is living a lie in every area of his life, he will eventually have to pay the price on some level.

Although the player is unconscious to the pain he causes, he realizes what he is doing. He may apologize and tell you he knows how difficult this is for you and that someday it will be different. He may even cry and tell you how miserable he is and how he wishes he met you all those years ago instead of being stuck with "her." You then feel sorry for him and try to help him sort out his life. You are understanding and give him space and time.

It must be hell to live in a world of constant stress, where he is constantly lying to everyone. What is worse is that he lies so much to everyone that even he does not know the truth anymore. The situation escalates. It becomes a bigger mess because everyone knows something, but no one is exactly sure what they know. The wife becomes suspicious and may tell his mother and her family members, hoping to gain comfort and "false" assurance. She wants others to convince her she is wrong because "he would never be unfaithful to her." She then becomes frantic, altering her routine with him and may initiate sex more often with him or follow him around the house, trying to get attention from him. Nothing seems to work. Her emotions are unstable and she may take her anger and frustration out on the kids or any other obligation that chains her.

Your suspicion mirrors his wife's as you begin to realize you do not know the full truth about what is going on in his marriage. After a while you, too, begin to question every little thing because something does not feel right.

Even his kids suspect something, if they are young adults or older.

People at his work start to question him (in their minds) because he is constantly running here or there and uses work as his excuse to be with you.

His wife may call his job and ask about that board meeting last Wednesday that never took place. Before he knows it, he is in Charlotte's web and the black widows are closing in on him.

It must take a lot of energy to carry out his lives of deception. It wears him out and somewhere in his subconscious (where the place of guilt normally resides) he knows what he is doing. Eventually, when it becomes too much of a burden for him, something has to either implode or explode. Guess who gets booted out the door? Not the wife! Not the kids! Certainly not the job! You will have outlived your purpose and will be kicked to the curb. Again, only you can decide what is right for you.

The Prince's Prison

As we can see, the player's priority is to protect and preserve his own interests. Unfortunately, the tangled web he weaves can be painful for all parties involved and, much like wives and mistresses, the pressure may drive him to do unthinkable acts. It can have devastating consequences that destroys many lives. In the past fifteen years there has been a plethora of men who have killed their mistresses, wives, and (even) children.

Again, the choices we make determine the kind of life we lead. If the player makes the choice to have sex with a woman and knowingly risks an accidental pregnancy, then he is responsible for his actions. He makes the choice to get married to a woman he may not love and then makes the choice to get involved with other women. He creates his own misery of lies and deceptions that will eventually come back to haunt him.

Let us expand on this point. These are dangerous men because, as they jump in and out of pillars, they have the uncanny ability to become whatever they must become at the moment to get what they want, much like (again) the car salesman. It is impossible to determine who they are at times because they act the part of whatever person they need to become. If they want to pose as the faithful loving husbands, for instance, they know what to say to their wives to get pity and sympathy from them. If they want to string their mistresses along, they know how to be calculating and cunning so that these naïve women fall for their lines of *bullshit*. The player is whatever the moment needs him to be. He is a con artist.

The danger arises when he has webbed such a fine web of deceit that he can't stand the pressure. And since he usurps personal responsibility for everything he does, he can become dangerous. Once a woman realizes the liar he truly is, she reacts negatively toward him and this makes him angry. If his ploys fail to charm her, he may use passive-aggressive behaviors to get even with her and all those he perceives as doing him wrong. Further, he does not accept responsibility for sleeping with another woman the night before, and perhaps this is what pissed off his wife to the *nag* point. In his mind, the wife should just accept his excuse and shut up. If she continues, he may get even with her in various ways that really ignite her anger in an attempt to retain his power and control. He knows the buttons to push. If the pattern continues, he may grow to resent her for holding him back from his own happiness. Add financial pressures and other demands and you have an explosion waiting to happen. He may feel (without remorse) he would be better off if she were dead. This is when his face is plastered all over the news for doing the unthinkable.

Circles and Triangles

Later in this book we are going to discuss ways to avoid men with such destructive traits. Once you are already involved, it is difficult to escape from this type of prison. And it is a prison. If we look at the dynamics of his set up, we can define it in geometrical terms. He has a large circle with his wife, as circles are indicative of marital relationships. While he is having an affair with you, he has a difficult time figuring out where to put you, assuming he has great feelings for you and that there are no other women floating in his web somewhere. Therefore, he creates a triangle that is vested inside of the circle. The triangle includes his wife, you and himself.

Before we continue, it is important to note that it is impossible to have more than one intimate, emotional relationship at a time. We can have sexual relations with various partners and may love them, but the deep emotional connection is usually generated with one person. It is the scientific Principle of Superposition that says no two things can occupy the same place at the same time. If this principle is applied to our conversation, we can say that love is not a thing but a feeling, which takes up space of its own kind and cannot be compartmentalized in a pillar.

Time, however, is the determining factor. When you are together having an intimate time with your player, you draw closer in emotional proximity; his connection and emotions are vested with you. After he leaves you, he is in the afterglow, which takes a few days to evaporate. When he leaves and returns to his wife, she feels his distance, and may "nag" and scratch for his attention, which pulls him from his afterglow with you. This makes him distance himself and recoil in the *guilt space* of hibernation. Then he retreats to his wife, makes up with her, and the connection you had with him three days ago is gone. You are now scratching. Given some time, he will cut that connection with her and return to you.

These connections are deep rooted and are impossible to miss when they disappear. This is what creates tumultuous confusion and chaos in the player's world. He becomes frustrated because both his wife and mistress are acutely aware of when the connection is lost, thus he feels pressured to give what he does not have at the moment. The player is living in a love triangle while he shuffles from each corner, like a ping-pong ball, all while trying to live peacefully in the circle with his wife.

Rise and Crash

This triangular pattern is what causes deep emotional scars in all parties involved. There is no stability whatsoever with a man who cultivates relationships with more than one partner. The mistress, for example, floats in the afterglow of their wonderful time together after (he built) the emotional connection with her that rose to the top. She becomes elated from their emotional-high connection but then when he leaves, he cultivates the relationship with his wife and abandons his mistress. This is essential if he wants to maintain his circle. The mistress, therefore, crashes to the ground as he deprives her. His wife experiences the same wreck as she believes on a Saturday night that her husband truly is faithful to her and then puts her suspicions in the *ridiculous* box, only to crash Monday from emotional deprivation when he abandons her. She wonders where his emotional connection went as he stops confiding in her and stays late at work all week. He does not want to eat when he comes home or may go straight to bed. It is very painful. The player has the best of the situation because abandonment does not touch his world. Either the wife or the mistress is meeting his needs while being abandoned most of the time. He may eventually fall at his own hands and, as he deserves, end up alone.

The Walls of the Prison

Dost thou know the pain he hath caused?
Wherefore dost thou leave me to love another?

9

Waiters and Watchers

No matter how we define it or explain it, being a mistress is not the most flattering position in which a woman can put herself. It is no picnic being the wife of an unfaithful man, either. Both can become victims of the many interactions he generates in those thick pillars. The mistress is what I call the *waiter* and the wife is, to no surprise, the *watcher*.

Before we exemplify this point, we must, again, remember that women put themselves in situations. If the mistress defines her role and is agreeable to the terms of the arrangement, she will not become emotionally invested. Therefore, she will experience very little pain. Most women, however, do not set boundaries for themselves or for their players. Instead, they make assumptions about where the affair is headed. This is what gets them into trouble.

I call the mistress a *waiter* because the majority of her time she spends alone, waiting on his call, his arrival, and his schedule that determines the specifics of their next meeting. The woman on the side is continually in the closet, taking a back seat to his wife. It is a lonely, dark existence when she wants to radiate with love, companionship and togetherness. She wants a partner, a best friend, a companion with whom she may build a life, a husband (in most cases). The problem is that he already has a wife. As defined earlier, the arrangement in which she put herself is an affair, not a relationship.

An affair offers no equal ground right from the start because the mistress is free and the player is tied to someone else. He has total control because he sets the schedules for their dates, telephone calls and correspondence. If he calls her on his way home from work and she is tending to something else, she will not connect with him that day. She must reschedule and plan around his time table or wait until the following day. This is contrary to the equal relationship when she would return his call when she is ready. By the time she is ready to return his call, he is busy with his wife and, most likely, children. This minimizes her power and puts him in total control.

After a while, the affair becomes old and generates an enormous amount of resentment. The mistress becomes increasingly resentful of the hurried love sessions and becomes irritated at his continual lies. Should she make scornful comments about his wife and marriage, he retorts in defense and will most likely make the mistress very angry. She becomes resentful that he keeps her in the closet and lacks the courage to tell his wife the truth. This is when the "other woman" realizes he may not want to tell his wife the truth. His wife comes first and calls all the shots, as she might see it, and this is unacceptable to her. Although she put herself in this situation and is not entitled to anything, she begins to "hate" the wife and everything that takes him away from her. She fantasizes about walking in his house together with him while he tells her that she is the one with whom he wants to spend his life. These thoughts are derived from desperation, and the logical mistress knows somewhere in her heart that these sentiments are irrational. She is in *mistress prison.*

Harsh reality has it that his wife (in most cases) is not the "bitch" she wants her to be, and the mistress knows in her heart (even if she denies it) that he is the one who keeps himself with his wife. He gives her the power and control, either out of desire or fear, to hold him. The truth is that his wife is in the same prison of darkness, only she does not know the circumstances surrounding her. She (most likely) does not know who the mistress is or if there is a mistress, but she knows something is wrong.

The wife is what I term the *Watcher.* Don't think she doesn't sniff his clothes after he has been with his mistress or check his car for evidence while he is in the shower. And those cell phone calls? She is frantically searching for the identity of the woman who is *stealing* her husband. This woman becomes obsessed and watches every single thing her husband does, all while living in the same constant panic (as the mistress does) while she is waiting for him. She is scared to confront him or question him because she fears he will lie to her and then accuse her of being crazy, just like poor Alice. She is in *wife hell.*

Circling the Airport

If you are a mistress and you realize your affair is not going anywhere, then your plane will not crash (metaphorically speaking). If you are grounded and do not have grandiose expectations, then you will not board the plane. If, however, you want much more from your player and he knows you want more, he is apt to make false promises that will hurt you in the long run. He may ask you to be patient for a little while longer, but that *little while longer* turns into an eternity. This man may tell you what you want to hear while whispering sweet nothings in your ear or purport that he is divorcing his wife in six months, perhaps right after the youngest child turns eighteen-years old. Before you know it, six months has turned into six years and the eighteen-year old just graduated from college. Several years later you finally realized that your plane never left the ground. The moment of reality hits you. You wonder where you were every time the plane circled the airport. You wonder how you did not see his circular motion. You spent two years with this man in a holding pattern at the airport while he gave you the appearance all along that you were going to take off.

He bought the tickets, you had your bags packed, and all the while there are reasons, excuses everyday why the plane never left the ground. You have been patient and understanding. He is clever and knows how to keep you obediently in his pillar. All you have to do is wait a little bit longer, right? Wrong! Now, this morning you just came to the realization that you will never fly above where you are right now.

Free Pass to Disneyland

If you are a mistress involved with another woman's husband or a wife married to an unfaithful man, I would bet you are both devoted to him. Keep in mind, however, that players love fun, enjoyment and excitement.

The mistress makes him feel adored and, realistically, he gets great sex (for free) from her. She gives him a free year's pass or sometimes two or three year's pass to Disneyland. This man comes and goes whenever he pleases and then leaves by the end of the day. The player owes you (the mistress) nothing, and he gives only surface things that have nothing to do with *forever*. It is ecstasy of the here and now that has no promise of anything other than the present moment.

If this arrangement is mutual, then you have not lost the *forever* for which many women may long. The player comes to have fun for one day and then returns home to his reality where his commitments are rooted. Notice I said *commitments*. You are his pleasure without cost. He owes you nothing because you are aware that he belongs to another woman and you are agreeing to this arrangement by sleeping with him anyway. If the relationship progresses and you employ *wifely* demands with which he is all too familiar at home, he may begin to treat you with the same disrespect as his wife. If you begin to nag and question him, as he may perceive, you become an obligation.

If you are the wife, however, you are busy holding down the fort at home with the kids, the house, and the family duties, while he is having fun at Disneyland with another woman.

Since this book is about information and enlightenment, it is fair to say that the choices we make and the treatment we accept determine the kind of life we lead. It is your choice.

I'm Trapped and Can't Get Out

Unfortunately, once you are seduced into this world, he makes it next to impossible for you to escape. It is much like Cinderella when the handsome Prince gives her the opportunity to escape the evil stepmother. How on earth could she ever pass this up? In many cases, women have fallen prey to men that orchestrate the affair so that they are entirely dependent upon them. If you are involved with a married man, there may be a chance that he has set it up so well for himself that you cannot escape him. I am talking about money, honey. I am very acquainted with a young lady who came to the United States from a country in South America. She had two small children at the time and was selling ice cream in a park to survive. Along came Mr. Right who was wealthy in finances, distinguished in features and charming to say the least, but he was also married with three children and had a dependent wife that never worked a day in her life. This meeting turned into a five-year affair. He gave her $8,000 a month and paid for her children to go to Catholic school. He bought her a car and was instrumental in helping her obtain American citizenship. How could she afford to give this up? What was her alternative?

At first, this arrangement met both of their needs. As the affair escalated, however, he became more possessive and demanding. She was suffocating from his domineering personality and poor treatment of her. He controlled her every move, which is not surprising because he lured her in by taking care of the *damsel in distress* that she was. Again, players love power and control over the "weaker" woman, which gives them total domination. This young lady was lured into a situation that provided her with financial stability and comfort, and she had no choice but to stay with him because she was a (financially) "poor" undocumented illegal with children who was struggling to survive. Essentially, she was his prostitute. He owned her, all the while he was a "devoted" husband to a woman he married twenty-five years prior.

As the affair progressed, she put pressure on him to leave his wife. "If you love me as you proclaim, then leave her and marry me." Yes, this is a logical demand, given he set up the situation to make her think she was his "only love." It was evident the woman was in love with him, but he was killing her feelings. The more she pushed, the more he pushed back. The affair escalated to violence. When she terminated the affair, he used all means to keep her under his thumb. She grew to resent him but continued to take him back because she needed him. It was a dysfunctional cycle that left her feeling used, abused and worthless. The worst part about this picture was that he was actually very much in love with her. I happen to know without a doubt that she was the love of his life, and he became blindly obsessed with her. Fearing he would lose too much money, he was too cowardly to tell the truth to his wife. He continued to live the lie and the status quo; consequently, everyone lost.

If a man is holding you hostage in this type of affair, the best way to escape is to plan an exit from him. This exit requires careful planning. If you stash money away and explore higher education opportunities, you will have a safety net. You may want to network with the financial aid department at a local community college and explore your options and available resources. You may also network with business people or those in the same industry. The key is to build relationships. Devise goals that will help you meet your deadline. Things do not change unless changes are made. The best advice I can give is use him as he uses you. If he will pay for your education, let him do it. If you are going to have to stay with him anyway, as was the case of this young lady, then at least stay with an exit plan in mind. After all, he was the one who courted you, pursued you, tempted you and supplied you with all that you need. This may have been an acceptable set up for a while but, if you now want more, it is time to look out for yourself.

The Stand Off

In my own best interest, I am escaping the prison. I am worth a million hearts in gold, and I choose to be the only Queen.

10

The Drawbridge

If you were a single maiden in medieval times, you would have become all too familiar with the drawbridge. The drawbridge moved up or down, depending on the scope of the danger lurking. No matter what, it functioned as a means to either keep others out or to "shut you in." It was a protective mechanism. If you are in a hurtful affair with a married player, you must build your own drawbridge. Eventually you will either eliminate him from your life or recoil inside of yourself while planning an exit.

You will eventually get to the point where you will either have to force change or risk being abandoned. If you keep allowing him to come and go, he will lose respect for you and may rekindle with his wife or someone else, all while stringing you along. You may then begin to hound him to the *pain in the ass* point of no return. If you know he is deceiving you, it may become too difficult to continue on the same path and pretend that you are not suspicious, angry or resentful. You have two

choices: leave him or keep him. If you keep him, you have to be
willing to accept that he may not give you anything other than
what he is giving you now. Unless he confesses to his wife and
makes the choice to divorce her, the same pattern will emerge.
The definition of insanity is when we repeat the same patterns
and expect different outcomes. It simply does not work. Many
women choose to remain in the situation while nagging him to
change. If this applies to you, know that this tactic forces you to
expend more energy and only hurts you because he will then
run back to his wife for solace from your *pain in the ass* nagging,
as he did to her when he was first running to you. The cycle
will continue.

For every action you take, there is a consequence or a
reward. You are in charge of your own destiny. If you put
yourself in this situation, you can get yourself out of it. The key
is to step back and avoid acting impulsively. My grandmother
used to say, "Haste makes waste." I prefer to go one step
further and say that haste makes hell. When you are
emotionally triggered, it is easy to fly off the handle and react in
a manner that harms you. The last thing you want to do is
orchestrate a situation where you generate more pain for
yourself than you have already had. Let us discuss your options
and examine the outcomes that your actions might produce.

Burning Down the Kingdom

After circling the airport for years and holding up

Disneyland for your married player, you are bound to escalate
to the point of nuclear explosion, especially if you want more
than he is offering. This is when the situation can become
dangerous to you. You may start to feel unworthy, resentful,
and hateful. If you realize that his relationship with his wife is
much more than he portrayed, you will most likely feel
betrayed, used, cheated and stupid. This is when you fantasize
about calling his home or taking a nice trip to see his wife. At
this point, you must step back, pause and recharge before acting
impulsively. Pull up the drawbridge, honey. Remember: Haste
makes a *hellish waste*.

A perfect example of the nuclear explosive point is the
climax of the movie *Fatal Attraction* when Glenn Close boils a
rabbit on the stove in his home to get even with him. Another
example, real life, is that of Amy Fischer who shot Joey
Buttafucco's wife, Mary Jo, in the face as she answered the door.
These are examples of pure insanity and carry with them serious
consequences. No matter how angry you are, it pays to remain
calm. The question I must ask: Is any man worth giving up
your soul and spending the rest of your life in prison? Choose
wisdom before pride, honey!

Before we continue, we must explore two important things:
If you have become so involved with any man that you
relinquish complete control of your emotions, then you must
step back and analyze your emotional dependence. It is

dangerously unhealthy. The second point is that you must examine what you want in the long run and determine the best route to get there. You are responsible for your own actions, feelings and behaviors. Rule the rage, don't let the rage rule you!

If you want a stable, secure relationship with a faithful man, you must accept reality that you do not have a faithful man in your player. He may not have the qualities you need to give you what you want. If he is cheating on his wife, then he is a cheater. Do you want a cheater? Do you want to be his queen while he is out with another princess? He cannot even offer his own wife a stable, secure, and faithful relationship. Do you expect him to behave differently with you? Examine this point and focus on the glorious future that is waiting for you. Detach his behaviors from your own self worth and focus on improving yourself.

The next unwise choice the mistress makes is confessing all to his wife. She wants to knock on the door and bombard her with an avalanche of information that will completely destroy his life. This grandiose scheme does not work most of the time and it may even backfire in many ways. Again, ask yourself what you want in the long term and if the actions you take will get you there.

If you make the choice to visit his wife, then you may want to explore all possible outcomes ahead of time. Will she, in turn, react in haste and cause irreversible damage to you or to him? To what degree are you familiar with her mental and emotional stability? If she is sane, you may get the opposite of what you had hoped. Chances are you would be doing her a big favor because after he tells her that you meant nothing to him and now he knows for sure that he loves her more than ever, she is in *wife heaven*. This woman has waited all these years for him to finally realize she is the one he wants and may use this as leverage to make him crawl back to her thinking he has finally learned his lesson. She may forgive him, and their marriage may become better than ever. Until the next one comes along, that is. In the meantime, you have been kicked to the curb as some transitional person who has led him to his (temporary) true spiritual transformation and growth. The only person who gets hurt most of the time is the other woman.

If you are contemplating this course of action, you might not want to waste your energy. We will discuss something that will work like a charm and will get you what you need in the long run.

Smoke Him Out

One interesting point to reiterate about players is that, again, they rarely take action unless forced to do so. If he has a comfortable life at home, why would he want to leave his wife? This point is especially true if you are holding up Disneyland, allowing him to come and go as he pleases. The truth that a mistress may not want to face is that the man is just not willing to leave his wife. He is not willing to put himself in an uncomfortable position by breaking his commitment to her to foster one with you. That is the bottom line. As we discussed earlier, the player lives in constant fear of disapproval and lives his life on the edge. In fact, this secret affair with you may be his adrenaline rush that he enjoys. He chases the *high* of danger.

The best tactic to take with a married man who will not make up his mind and continually runs home to his safe haven is to do nothing at all, absolutely nothing. Sounds too simple and definitely not tortuous enough, but trust me, it works. Smoke him out and wait. Even the dumbest creatures in a cave know enough to rise to the surface when there is smoke. Where there is smoke, there is fire, and this means danger. The last thing this man may want to do is lose the good thing he has with you. Make him rise to the surface and watch what he does.

Once you have more of a relationship with yourself and focus on you (not on him), he will begin to notice changes, sort of like the changes you notice when he is reconnecting with his wife again. Your emotional dependence should come from within you. If you become totally self reliant, you will be the boss of you, not he. The best way to begin the process of improvement is to plan ahead. Take out your project planner and plan an event for each night of the week: go to a movie, a church event, a friend's house, a support group advertised in the newspaper, or anything that seems interesting. Whatever you do, keep busy. Apply for a second job or enroll in a college course. Do something productive that forces you to engage with other people and offers you a chance to further your progress. Plan your future. Find your passion that will, perhaps, secure your financial resources: art, drama, poetry, or any other activity that sparks your interest. When you become first priority in your life, it will not matter as much that he does not make you a priority at all.

The longer you have been with this man, the more he knows your patterns, and the more you matter to him. Married men do not keep women for long periods of time if they are *not that into them.* Two years is about right, three at the most. If he keeps you longer than this, he is more emotionally involved than he may think. If this speaks to you, control the self talk that goes on in your mind and release your fear of his abandonment. He may be back faster than usual if your independence threatens him. If he does not return, good riddens!

Remember that he has you in his life for a reason (because it is all about him), and you give him something he needs. If you have been with him for several years, the chances are very likely that he cannot function peacefully without. In fact, when you are not in his life, it may make his poor wife's life more unbearable. If he cannot stand being away from you, he may start picking at everything in his home and begin to circle like a caged cat in heat.

When he starts getting frustrated and confronts your possible abandonment of him, avoid the famous *nag* talks that we women sometimes have with men, talks that put their ears on mute while they pretend to listen. Say vague things like, "I've noticed you have been preoccupied lately, and I don't want you to be miserable at home. Maybe you need some space to figure out what makes you happy." His reaction will be loaded with confusion and desperation. This is the last thing he wants. He is used to hounding, nagging questions: "Why didn't you call me? Where have you been?" Put the shoe on the other foot and watch him "hop along" by withholding information. See how he likes it.

No matter what you decide, be consistent. Contemplate long and hard about what you really want. If you take him back into your arms right away, be aware that your situation may worsen because he did not have to work hard to get you back where he wants you. He may lose respect for you because you are not firm in your boundaries. Should your mind be set on having this man for good, make sure you have firm guidelines for what you are willing to accept, and then make him wait. Imposing the time sanction can do wonders because men hate to wait. This may take six months. Also, be prepared that this may not turn out like you had hoped. Whatever the case, it will turn out the way you need for your peace of mind.

If you want him to divorce his wife and commit to you, then go beyond the "needing space" comment. Say something like, "I've been doing a lot of thinking lately. You have so much on your plate with your wife and kids. I've hardly seen you, and you seem to be overwhelmed. You may need some space to figure out which direction your life is taking. Our relationship (the way it is) does not seem to meet your needs, and I am looking at what meets my needs. I need space to find out what kind of relationship I want. A man that is committed to a wife and kids is not a prospect for a committed relationship. Call me when you have an idea what you want, and if I am still available, we will renegotiate our terms." When you speak to him, avoid emotion. Men are turned off by overactive, emotional women. A confident, determined woman always rises to the top and obtains her goals by *not* reacting.

When he calls you in a week, cut the conversation short and avoid his calls for a while. Be as gone to him as he has been to you over the years. Take the control and power he has had over you and, quite frankly, shut down Disneyland. Make it so he has to circle the airport with one shoe on and the other off. If this man truly loves you, you will notice changes in his behavior. He may begin to behave like a starving dog in a steakhouse parking lot. If he begs, don't negotiate with him. Tell him you have said what you needed to say. The more persistent he is, the more he is rising to the surface. He may begin to panic at the thought of losing you for good.

Orchestrate a situation that is right for you, no matter what the outcome. Be honest and forthright. Your goal should also be to eradicate the deception and break out of the closet. Truth be told: He should not be deceiving his wife. If he truly loves you, he should stop living a lie with his wife. He should give her a chance to find real happiness with someone else. If he truly loves his wife, he should not be chasing after you or anyone else. Most importantly, your goal should be to adhere to a set of principles that enhances your worth. This means entering into a mutual relationship (absent all pillars) where you are the only woman.

When he pursues you, hold to your values and principles. Mean what you say, and say what you mean. Make it harder for him to see you. Avoid having sex or intimacy with him. The temptation may arise because you will want him in your arms and your bed again. If you give into him, chances are great that you will not get what you want. You will have given away your power (or what little power you once had). If he comes back to you and says that he is willing to leave his wife, ask for the divorce papers. Remember that he has cleverly learned how to manipulate you with words and will tell you anything you want to hear. Keep in mind also that you want a husband, and he already has a wife on whom he is presently cheating. Again, the choice is yours.

If he does not come back to you, then do not waste your time. I know that sounds painful, but do you want a man that does not love you enough to commit to you? Have you depleted all your energy keeping Disneyland up and running? Do you want to continue circling the airport for the next ten years? You will never get off the ground if you do not make changes.

If he comes back to you and is willing to take action and give up everything for you, trust him. He took "painful" action for you, which is highly unusual. I must stress, however, if there are kids involved, especially small ones, you will probably lose no matter what. It is the money, honey. Most men fear losing their paychecks and would much rather suffer in the home rather than risk losing the green. It is also difficult for anyone to leave their children. If he is willing to abandon his children for you, you may want to think twice about this man. Notice I said "abandon," not divorce. There is a huge difference. If you do end up with this man, then you must also welcome his children into your world together and be kind to them. To do otherwise would be to abandon the kids and this would set them up for a lifetime of pain. An honorable woman understands this.

Before you make your decisions, be aware of what you are able to give. You may also lose if he has a manipulative, conniving wife to whom he was married for years. She may

scheme and manipulate him in various ways because she knows
his weaknesses and may play on his guilt to get him back.
Unfortunately, many second marriages are destroyed because of
this very problem. It is not the ex-wife's behavior that causes
the destruction, but it is the husband's guilt and inability to set
firm limits with the "ex" that causes the problems. You need not
worry about this right now because chances are likely that he
will stay right where he is and wallow in self-pity until he finds
another woman to provide Disneyland for his escape.

Either way, you will be the winner. Hold firmly to what you
want. If your goal is to find an available man who commits to
you, it will either be him or a single man that will appreciate
you. Your other option is to stay in this prison for the next
fifteen or twenty years, or until his smallest child reaches
adulthood. Then, however, he may have another excuse for
why he absolutely cannot leave his wife: she has malignant
cancer or the house burned down or there was a death in the
family.

Courage of a Queen

When addressing the mistress, I do not wish to minimize the
pain of the queen. The players' actions are simply wrong and
inexcusable and, not because society deems it wrong, but for the
mere fact that it hurts. It hurts like hell. It is wrong to make
someone hurt. There are two different types of *Queen Prisons*, as
I call them. The first prison is when the wife suspects her

husband is having an affair but has no proof until she catches him red-handed. It is much less painful when the wife has suspected for some time because, although she has not realized it, she has had time to start the grieving process, if merely on a subconscious level. She is more prepared for the reality when it hits her. It is disastrous, however, in the second prison where the unsuspecting wife has her world turned upside down by his secret lives. This is dangerous.

If you are a suspicious wife seeking evidence that your husband is running around, you may want to put yourself on pause for a moment. If you do not have a scintilla of evidence, you run the risk of causing damage to your relationship if you react impulsively. A wise woman employs patience. You do not want to create a self-fulfilling prophecy where you drive him to an affair by willing it so. The first thing you may want to do is take inventory of your relationship and write down your suspicions. Keep a journal. Take the next step after patterns appear. You may want to avoid jumping to conclusions because his strange behaviors may have nothing to do with another woman. It may be something happening with his job or with some other area of his life that has upset him. Men need space to find solutions to figure things out.

The Suspecting Queen

If you have taken inventory and notice a pattern of strange happenings or if you have seen emails or text messages from other women (proof of his infidelity), then you may want to take inventory of your life. Before you approach him, know exactly what you want. You may not want to let him know that you are on to him until you have a clear direction. Turn his game back on him. Use his rules. He is the one who is deceiving you and by this point, you have nothing else to lose if you hold out a little longer. If he is truly in love with another woman, you must prepare yourself. Using threats and attempts to hold him may not work. Should you approach him, be aware that he may give into your ultimatums because he fears separation and abandonment, not necessarily because he loves you. He may want to stay with you where it is safe (his habit), rather than risk you walking out on him (abandonment) and tarnishing his reputation with family and friends. However, this is not love. You must decide if you want real love, or if you want to give him a second chance when the trust has already been destroyed. Remember: Repeat offenders often repeat the same offenses. Rarely do relationships recover once they have passed a certain point of betrayal, much like trying to mend a cracked egg shell. Many couples have gone into marriage counseling only to find it is a temporary fix and a year or two down the road, the same patterns emerge and the divorce is nastier than thought possible.

It is up to you. Once you take personal inventory, you may want to consult an attorney. Explore your legal rights. You may also want to explore your own financial situation. Do you have a career to which you can turn? If not, you may want to explore the possibility of higher education or training before you approach him and ask for a divorce. No matter what you decide, know that a wise woman explores all her options before she shows her hand. Know what you want for your future and explore how to get it. Further, you must understand that the only person you can control is you. No matter how hard you try, you will not be able to control him.

On a more hopeful note, if you have a man who truly loves you and may have strayed for *stupid reasons*, as he may claim, you may want to reevaluate the situation. Is the relationship worth saving? What was missing in your marriage that prompted him to stray? The only way to truly tell is by waiting it out and watching what happens. Again, if you approach him, he may panic and show his undying love to you. This may be his momentary truth that may not last. To avert the *bullshit*, as one woman so eloquently put it, she decided to hire a private investigator. Surprisingly enough, she was not seeking to quell her suspicions or gather proof of his infidelity; she needed to see pictures or something concrete to know if he was really in love with the other woman. A picture is worth a thousand words. A wise woman employs patience and explores all options before showing her hand.

An insecure woman may not want to give up an unfaithful

husband no matter what. *Do anything, but please don't leave me!*
This is unfortunate because her fear of abandonment is far
greater than her fear of being imprisoned in a loveless marriage.

I want to take a moment to discuss how this negative
situation affects the children, especially girls. I once heard of a
situation where a suspecting wife used her kids to get even with
her husband by calling their attention to his infidelity. Not only
did she get even with him, but she used them to control his
behaviors and make him *tow the line,* as she would purport.
Please know that no matter what situations we, as adults,
orchestrate for ourselves, it is our responsibility to protect kids,
not to draw them into our drama. Some may deem it
reprehensible that this woman watched her husband get ready
to leave for work on Valentine's Day and, in suspect that he
would see his mistress later that day, yelled to her daughters,
"Look, girls, Daddy has a girlfriend!" The girls, preteens at the
time, turned in silent terror, not knowing what to say. Keenly
aware that he was committed to his kids, this suspecting wife
was sure that her comment would upset her husband enough to
cancel any plans he had (with his mistress) later and race home
to have it out with her about the incident. And she was right.

This woman was willing to create an argument in order to
keep him home, much like many players create fights to get
away. Further, she was willing to risk the esteem of her
daughters and call attention to the fact that their "Daddy" was

unfaithful, which put them in a terrible position. As we will discuss further, girls will eventually seek men like their fathers. Some would ponder how this woman could jeopardize her daughters in such a way. Further, the player is at fault, too, because he "played into his wife's manipulation," allowing her to control the entire situation. At the same time, he lacked the balls to be honest with his wife. By running home and calling attention to his wife's comment, he was teaching his wife how to get what she wanted next time, all while continuing to perpetuate the lie.

Some women find it difficult to act in their best interest or in the best interest of their children, which is unfortunate because they are showing their kids how to repeat the cycle of pain and destruction. Had this woman really wanted the truth, she would have taken action to find it, all while leaving her kids out of the equation.

The Unsuspecting Wife

The most painful situations in which a woman can find herself is that of a wife who one day realizes her husband has been running around. As far as she is concerned, there were no warning signs. One day her life is turned upside down and then destroyed. This woman has a serious choice to make. She can accept the situation and focus on herself, or she could throw her energy into inflicting harm on him. Both choices are unbecoming while battling the storm.

If you are a scorned wife, you know what I mean. There is no such thing as *thinking clearly* when your entire world has been turned upside down and thrown into tumultuous chaos. It is like being sucked into the eye of a slow-whirling hurricane because the one person you trusted and depended on emotionally has betrayed you in the worst manner possible. You feel like a fool. The fact that he kept it secret while you (his unsuspecting wife) continued to pour energy into him makes you angrier than the actual adultery. "If only he had been honest with me."

No matter how we look at it, an unfaithful husband is most dastardly and reprehensible. It is difficult to overcome from his betrayal, but all wounds heal with time. Each day the pain will ease some more, and you will eventually become strong again. You must now muster the strength to make decisions that will bring you joy, not more pain.

Forever Mine, Faithfully

The most contented hearts radiate love's light.

11

The Diamond Ring

If you want a faithful man, you must first be faithful to
yourself. Whether you are a mistress who is involved with a
"taken" man or a wife married to a man who makes it with the
ladies, you have soul searching to do. Start by taking a good
look in the mirror and acknowledge that beautiful woman.
Nurture her and do not let him use her or disrespect her in any
way. If you want a faithful man, then be true to yourself first.
Most importantly, be honest about your situation. You have
some important choices to make, but you first have to accept
reality. Your mate's infidelity is a reflection on him, not you.
The fact that you choose to stay with him may reflect the deeper
struggles with which you battle, but it is time to make tough
decisions. You will be in for more pain if you expect him to one
day change into a faithful, honorable man. The chances are
greater that he will not change, but you can.

If you have repeatedly chosen unfaithful, *bad boy* men, it is
time to figure out why. Examine the choices you have made in

your life and force yourself to feel the painful memories. If you can feel the pain, you can heal from it. This takes courage, commitment and support. You may want to consider professional assistance that will help you dig into your past to explore your fears, anger and negativity that has led you to make the choices you have made.

There are alternate methods for healing the trauma (from betrayal and mistrust) that many claim work more quickly. Emotional Freedom Techniques (EFT), for example, help balance the energy systems comprised in the body's energy infrastructure. This is a fantastic method of drawing from the body the "stuck" energy by tapping on the essential chakras. Emotional Freedom Techniques help remove this heaviness, much like cleaning out a congested closet. This has been an excellent healing technique for Post Traumatic Stress Disorder (PTSD) for servicemen/women. It is so important that we clear old emotional wounds to release the depressed energy that holds us back. Once this heavy energy gets trapped within us, it affects every area of our lives. Unfortunately, we are not consciously aware that we bring this energy with us everywhere we go. This negative baggage makes our sadness so transparent. It turns people off.

Many women have found great relief from EFT and similar healing techniques. As you begin to clear your energy space, the energy to *come out of your shell* will slowly appear. You will then be free to explore numerous possibilities for personal and professional growth: You may want to build a social network and expose yourself to different people; you may want to visit a college campus and talk to an academic advisor; you may want to explore different career possibilities. Whatever you do, make it a priority to take charge of your life.

In order to come out of your shell and take risks, you have to feel secure and confident. This is difficult when you have been torn apart by betrayal. Your drawbridge is hooked too tightly to your wall within. The depressed energy dampens your spirit and makes it next to impossible to renew your life. Again, you must remove your negative baggage to make room for the positive. Free up your closet and throw out all the things that are just taking up negative space in your life.

Many people simply do not know how to do this and spend years in a robotic life going through the motions without every really experiencing it. They cling to the "bitter" past mistakes that were made: "If only I could go back in time!" Get over it. Reality is such that you can't go back in time. Stop wasting your energy on what could have been. The only choice you have is to charge ahead with dignity and pride. Proceed with determination to change your life for the positive.

Once you clean out the heavy negative energy, you can begin to change the way you think. This will bring self confidence. For example, you may need to retrain your patterns

of thinking so that your thoughts are consumed with positive
self images. Painful situations of betrayal and mistrust do more
damage than we even realize because, in a sense, it is mind
control. Our minds become like broken tapes that keep
repeating how worthless we are if "he" does not want us.

Remember that a little girl is conditioned that she must have
a man to love her; otherwise, she is unworthy. Once you change
the way you think, you will change the way you behave.
Eventually, you will begin to take risks and assume the skills to
draw to you quality men that will not betray you.

The law of attraction asserts that you get back what you
give out. If you are a free spirit with positive energy and vibrant
light, you will radiate and attract the same in return. A negative,
depressed person, however, is unapproachable because she is
stuck in heavy energy. This is understandable, especially when
she has been through such hard times. It is a lot like someone
bursting into the room where you are now and abruptly
punching you in the stomach. When you are knocked to the
ground, you have to catch your breath and gather your
composure. Obviously, you are hurting, throbbing, and need
time to heal, which is no different than if someone "knocks the
shit out of you" emotionally. The difference is you cannot see it
with the visible eye because the bruises are on the inside. It is a
terrible cycle that demands strength, enlightenment and
support. If a woman has been betrayed badly, she may be

terrified to ever risk loving again. Consequently, she spends the rest of her life in misery and the "bitchiness" comes out in a variety of ways. I have seen this happen many times. Naturally, it takes some women years to get over this, but they must first clean out the old baggage. It is now time to take inventory and fix your life.

Many women think that latching on to another man will fix the problem and the past will automatically disappear. This is, again, the *Cinderella Syndrome*, or the *fairytale wanting*. The old baggage from old wounds will begin to surface again and again. No matter where we go, there we are and so are all of our past experiences. You have to fix what is wrong in order to make things right. Do not look to a man to save you. This is probably how you attracted such a dastardly character in the first place.

The Bar Stools

I know so many women who have had such bad experiences with unfaithful men that they have given up on love all together. They do not believe there are any guys that can remain faithful. This is partly true, but not all men are unfaithful: some are and some are not. You attract to you what you are, both consciously and subconsciously. It is now time to change.

Many women are unaware that their low self-esteem prevents them from feeling worthy of good men. The women that have always chased the *bad boys* and the unfaithful players simply do not know what to look for in good men. When they do bump into the faithful type, they find them incredibly boring and reject them. The good ones slip away.

When I was an undergraduate in college, my initial psychology class provided fascinating information that has served me quite well. The professor showed a short documentary that could not have explained any clearer the point I am now making. He first started by explaining what I will coin as *The Barstool Theory*. Let us say a woman walks into a bar and spots two sets of barstools, one on the right side of the bar and the other on the left side. The moment she enters the bar, her subconscious tapes (of all prior experiences) immediately scan the bar for that which is familiar to her. She zooms in and sizes a man up within thirty seconds, seeking a man with whom she is most comfortable. His looks, demeanor, attire and posture all present an accurate package of who he is. This is *first impression thing* we learned in kindergarten while being trained to stay away from strangers. Unfortunately, people size us up in thirty seconds or so and, whether right or wrong, there is a certain subconscious stereotyping that goes on in the *cautious box* in our minds. It is a protective measure, but many women dismiss it. If a woman was raised by an alcoholic, abusive father, for example, who was a *cold- hearted bastard,* she may immediately spot the *bad boy* on the right side of the bar. His body language, clothing, and demeanor tell her what kind

of man he is. The scruffy, dirty, aggressive, *bad boy* body
language draws her attraction as she focuses on him, forsaking
all others. She will probably dismiss the attorney (in the tailored
suite and friendly demeanor) on the left side of the bar who
"appears" gentle, respectful, educated and honorable. This guy
may intimidate her and, should she give him a chance, she may
sabotage anything potentially "good" with him. What is so
dangerous about this is that it all happens on a subconscious
level, like breathing air.

My goal is to bring your attention to this so that you can
begin to change your life. If you ever go into another bar, leave
the aggressive *bad boy* alone on his stool. If he looks like he will
not take a sassy word from anyone and will throw the first
punch, he probably will and it might be at you. Leave him right
where he is and, for the sake of wise choices, leave the attorney
alone, too, until you figure out who you are first. Then scope
him out and get to know who he is before jumping head over
heels into the flame of desire with him. Decide if he is worth
what you have to offer, not the other way around. Most
importantly, do not rush in and buy the car. If you did not have
a good father role model, then you probably make poor choices
in men. Now is the time to put the brakes on and tune into your
inner GPS.

If you want the diamond from an honorable man, then you
must look for a faithful one who puts his energy into making

you his wife. Here are some pointers to guide you.

A faithful man wants a woman who is her own person, a woman of confidence, purpose and direction. Do you have interests of your own? Do you have your own goals that you want to accomplish? Are you positive, alive and full of life? Do you hold yourself in high regard and seek to live life to the fullest? Do you laugh a lot and see the glass half full?

If you have been scorned badly and never worked through the trauma, you probably cry much more than laugh. This is understandable. Now, however, you must learn to release the negative baggage you are carrying because it is destroying you. The inner pain, neglect, abandonment, and abuse are all part of the baggage that steals your happiness. This makes you suffocate on your own pain. This heavy energy of unhappiness is so transparent that it can turn people off, especially good men. It is time to heal the pain and lighten your energy.

This type of man also respects a woman who respects herself. Do you set limits and boundaries that will make him toe the line and treat you with dignity, respect and honor? If you said yes, then his needs will not surpass your own. For example, if your date stands you up or does not follow through with plans, then the next night when he calls, tell him you are busy and that you will not be seeing him all week. When he calls the following evening, say "I realize you were busy last night and forgot our date. I hope everything is okay at work. Last night was the only night I had free to see you. I won't be seeing you this week because I am backlogged with things I have to do." And mean it! Make him sorry he missed you. You will mean more to him, and he will not take for granted that you will always be there for him. He will toe the line next time. Here is a story that will surely put a smile on your face:

Princess Clara

Clara was a twenty-year old college student studying Liberal Arts. A handsome gentleman asked her on a date one Friday night. She spent time getting ready for her hot date and was anxiously awaiting his arrival, which was supposed to be at 7:00 p.m.. She sat patiently waiting at 7:00 p.m. and then 8:00 p.m. rolled around. By 8:30 p.m.. she assumed he was not interested. An hour later, however, he arrived with anticipation of the exciting evening. Clara did not mention his tardiness. They had a spectacular time and made plans for the following Friday at the same time.

Next Friday, the gentleman arrived on time and asked one of the girls to inform Clara he was waiting downstairs. Clara slowly perfected her appearance and meandered into the family room asking the girls to deal her a hand of cards. "You have a date, don't you?" The girls asked. Clara nodded and continued to play cards while keeping a sharp eye on the clock. She asked someone to inform her date that she would be down shortly. The young man grew impatient. At 9:00 p.m. she meandered downstairs, greeted her date and eagerly anticipated a fun evening. He looked at her in dismay. "You sure take a long time to get ready, Clara," he commented peevishly. She smiled and replied, "The next time we have a date, I expect that you will honor your commitment and arrive on time." He was never late again. They have been married for over fifty years.

A faithful man wants an independent woman who gives

him his freedom, but also gives him boundaries. Most importantly, *brevity is the soul of wit,* as William Shakespeare once wrote. The less you say in words and the more you show in actions, the more respect you will gain.

Unfaithful Sperm

I cannot think of one situation where a woman said she wanted to get married so that her husband would run around on her. We all hope for the fairytale man that will never stray. The mistress wants what the player's wife wanted when she married him, and what she cries herself to sleep for at night while he is out at a "work meeting" in his other woman's bed. If you are the other woman, can you honestly say that had he divorced his wife and took you on his white horse that you would not worry when he told you someday he had a meeting for work? We know what you are thinking, or should I say trying *not to think* of at this time. Are you thinking that he would not do that to you because you are *the one*? You are the one chosen woman that will keep him happy enough to never stray?

There have been situations where this has happened. I am aware of a woman that spent eight years as a mistress and finally smoked him out because she just could not stand it any longer. Although he had been a player for thirty years, there was something about her that he could not find in anyone else and, when she finally smoked him out, he popped up shortly after with "forever" in mind. When he finally decided that he wanted her, he was never unfaithful to her. He kept returning and, once he was hooked, never jumped bate.

Then again, I am aware of another woman who spent thirty-five years as a mistress and in the end he never left his wife. She made the remark that had he left his wife, she was still not sure he would have chosen her. This woman always put him before herself, and he did not respect her enough to take any action. This mistress, as are many others, was afraid to smoke him out because she feared he would not return. It is the *abandonment thing* again; therefore, she lacked the courage to set limits and boundaries with him.

It is so important that women clear out childhood baggage before searching for a man. Become a whole person before you become a partner so that you have something positive to give. Otherwise you run the risk of repeating the old negative patterns that destroyed you the first time around. If you come from a dysfunctional home and have had a painful childhood, then you are more prone to possess dysfunctional traits. Further, dysfunctional people are self centered and "needy." This is not good. Healthy men will run like hell away from you.

Again, men seek women who possess self confidence, clear purpose and direction. Honorable men seek reasonable partners in life who will tell them when they are being *assholes*. Ladies, I do not mean nagging, complaining, yelling or whining, either.

There are feminine skills I am going to share with you that will help you hone your *man catching* skills. If you want the diamond ring, then make your finger shine ahead of time.

To Have and To Hold

I was once envious of a college friend because she always seemed to get the "perfect" guys. The only problem was that she could not keep them. They repeatedly dumped her. Many women, like her, know how to get them, but when it comes to the *Have and to Hold*, they just cannot make them stay. Here are some pointers that will help you understand why.

First, wise women are aware that the controlling type of woman is often dumped or put on the back burner while he runs around. Assured men do not like to feel smothered and controlled. It is as simple as that. You need to give him space to be who he is. Most importantly, a self-assured woman knows how to make a man feel like a man. For example, if the electric socket gives out in the kitchen, an assured woman will ask her man if he needs her assistance in fixing the outlet. She understands that men are problem solvers and solution finders. If you let him find the problem, he will generate a solution. A wise woman gives him this much without "cutting off his balls." She avoids controlling him, like "he hasn't the good sense to think his way out of a paper bag," as one man I once heard comment. There is no need to tell the man to call an electrician before giving him the opportunity to fix the problem. If he needs to call an electrician, he knows how to dial telephone numbers.

Secondly, a man needs to be appreciated and recognized for what he does. If he fixes the outlet, a wise woman offers him praise and acknowledges that it took three hours from his Saturday off time. Moreover, she calls attention to the fact that he quickly learned the electric profession in a few hours, which saved two-hundred dollars from the family budget. If he needs to be a problem fixer and a solution finder, which he is by nature, then recognize him for the success he proves to be. Validate his efforts and clever solutions.

Thirdly, everyone needs to be appreciated and acknowledged for who they are as human beings. A clever woman knows how to bring out the best in a man by being the wind beneath his wings. Give him encouragement and show him you appreciate him. Go up to him and hug him for no other reason than you wanted to touch him. Make him feel manly and macho, and he surely will be your Tarzan swinging from a rope.

Fourth, an assured woman understands that when a man has a lot of space, he will eventually close the *space gap* himself. If you give him space to figure out his own problem and generate a solution, he will eventually return your way and open up to you. If you listen to him with "real" listening skills, you can call attention to his main concerns. Paraphrase and validate what he is saying: "What I hear you saying is that you are unhappy with x, y and z. Have you given any thought to your idea about moving y to v?" This type of validation gives him the freedom to explore his own solutions.

Finally, a bright woman understands that patience is a virtue, and it is the very cure to any problem. Remember, haste makes a hellish waste and will cause more problems in the long run. When in doubt, do nothing at the moment. The wise woman stands back and observes her situation before taking action. Should you nag, hound, or badger him into giving you what you want, you will push him into someone else's arms, or you will push him out of yours. Either way you are losing the ring.

Empty Uterus

This section is written for the mistress.

A desperate woman finds it difficult to continue in a dead-end situation with a married man for too long. Notice I said *desperate*. She becomes so tired of the affair *not going anywhere* and is unsure how to nudge him to get what she wants. She cannot go on with the way things are and (believes) she cannot go on without him. It is a hellish nightmare because she is emotionally invested and attached to a man that has her on a roller coaster ride. This is dangerous, especially if her child bearing years are slipping away. Contrary to burning down his kingdom, she may try to connive her way to get what she wants and, consequently, wrecks her own world. Much to her demise, she may blindly wrap herself into the fantasy that, if she became pregnant with his child, he will automatically leave his wife for her. She may believe he will sweep her away to live happily ever after, leaving his wife and kids behind. This scenario is a near-guaranteed failure.

Always keep your focus in mind. No matter how desperate you become, you must be realistic about your situation. If you push, connive, or manipulate, then you will lose. Do you really want to be saddled with a child and lifelong responsibilities that will make your life more difficult? Think about the unborn child for a moment. With all the turmoil, strife and pain in which you currently wallow, how will this affect your future baby, especially if the father does not want the child? Surely you must know how painful abandonment is because most women who put themselves in these situations have abandonment issues of their own. Do you want to sentence another human being to this kind of prison? Do you want to make a bad situation worse? Only you can stop the cycle.

Think about how your affair has wrecked your life and, if you are desperate, then it has wrecked your life in more ways than you know. Now try to reason for a moment. If a man is unwilling to commit to you, you will only make a bad situation worse, simply impossible, if you force him into a commitment by an unwanted pregnancy. Remember: A player will run like hell when boxed into a corner. He will jump into any pillar he can find to escape you. If you think you feel abandoned now, you will really feel the brush off if you purposely set him up and entrap him.

The quickest way to lose a married man is to intrude on his home. By purposely plotting and planning an unwanted pregnancy, you are intruding on his life. Therefore, do not intrude on his home. Let him intrude on his home by realizing (on his own) that he does not want to be there. If he does not realize this and is unwilling to make a change, you either must accept the affair for what it is, or you must force yourself to move on to a single man who wants to plant his seed in you, creating a mutually agreeable conception. The unborn child deserves this, and so do you.

Inside a Faithful Ring lies the Diamond in the Heart

I am always perplexed by a woman who says she wants an honorable man but she, herself, does not behave in honorable ways. If I may be crude, getting *knocked up* on purpose does not say much about a woman's character. If you are a self-assured woman who knows what you want, you will never entertain the thought of getting *knocked up* to keep a man. This is one sure way to knock yourself down. Remember your priorities. If you do not have any, then think about what they might be. What is most important to you? What is it that you want in your heart?

These questions apply to wives, as well as mistresses. I am

amazed at married women who panic when they feel they are
losing their husbands and, on many occasions, end up pregnant
with another child. Why would a woman open herself to more
turmoil and chaos in an *already unstable* marriage? We would
assume that if a marriage is on the rocks, a new baby will only
add more bumps. Matters of the heart, however, are not
reasonable. This is most unfortunate because the child is the one
who suffers. If we look at this logically, we can deduce that a
woman may become desperate, believing that a new baby will
restore emotional solvency to her marriage and restore her (once
strong) love. It would be a new beginning and all their marital
problems might disappear. The relationship will magically
transform into marital bliss.

It is not just the wives who become desperate. Surprisingly
enough, the unfaithful man panics as well. In many cases, if the
player has a vasectomy or a wife has her tubes tied, they will
end up adopting a child. Why would a man want another child
with a wife he is still screwing around on? Here we have a
scenario where a man is in a bad marriage, being unfaithful and
dishonorable, yet makes the decision to adopt another child
with a wife he does not want. In addition, he already has three
small children for whom he is responsible. I know of a man that
had a wife and a mistress and, all while he was whispering
sweet nothings in his "other" woman's ear, was visiting fertility
specialists, hoping to conceive another child with a wife he

could not stand. How sane is this?

This is the type of situation that some would call playing Russian roulette with the peace state of mind. It is a chaotic situation, and the kids are the ones who suffer in the long run because they mirror what happens in the home. If there is negativity, neglect and strife in the home, the kids may end up having serious problems in adulthood with socialization and academic performance. They may end up with serious deficits in coping skills and may someday have more trouble in society. They may even cause trouble for society, which is unfair to the general population. Think about this for a second. If children are raised in homes where there was much turmoil, deception, suspicions, lies and hostility, their needs were most likely deprived. They were probably neglected youngsters. This type of environment produces hostile kids who will treat the world as their parents treated each other. These are the angry offenders who fight the world and everyone in it. It is always sad to hear the childhood stories of violent offenders or serial killers in prison.

Further, when the desperate couple continues to have children, they are too unhappy, dysfunctional, and preoccupied to raise them "properly." Who ends up raising them? Think about this for a second. While the wife is obsessed with chasing after her husband's love, she consequently neglects her kids. She may become moody, depressed, or angry. She may have zero tolerance because her frustration level is at its maximum; thus, she becomes short-tempered and agitated. As a result of her unstable peace of mind, the chemicals in her brain may begin to fluctuate, possibly causing a serious chemical imbalance. This may cause a nervous breakdown. What does this do to the children? She may become abusive to the older kids and may neglect the small ones who are too young to fend for themselves. Therefore, the kids have too much to deal with, especially the older ones, because they are forced to become primary caregivers to the younger ones. In short, they are forced to become parents while they are still kids. How fair is this?

If you are a wife lingering in a difficult marriage, you may want to think twice before continuing to make unwise choices. You must remember that your self worth is not defined by your marriage or your "success" as a wife. Most importantly, your self worth should not be defined by whether or not your husband loves you.

I Do

A player once told me that many women, once married, lose sight of who they are and eventually become imposters. He said husbands wonder if it is PMS or mood swings or some form of illness that took their wives away. What he does not understand is that insecure women are miserable people. A Miserable woman in an insecure relationship becomes a miserable spouse. Her childhood baggage came with her to

adulthood and then right into her marriage. No surprise there.
Here are some pointers I am going to share with you in the most
didactic tone.

If women only knew just how much power and control they
have in relationships, they might use it to their advantage rather
than to their detriment. Whether or not we choose to admit it,
women have the power over which direction relationships take.
There is a scene in the movie *My Big, Fat Greek Wedding* that is
not only comical, but so true: "The man may be the head of the
house, but the woman is the neck, and she can turn the head any
way she wants." This is the truth. That being said, the wise
woman uses power to her advantage. If you choose a man who
has faithful traits and then nurture him, he will become more
faithful to you. If you show your mate that you value and
appreciate him and then validate his needs, he is more apt to
meet your needs in return.

You cannot have a strong partnership when one person is
hounding, nagging and putting you down all the time. You
cannot have a partnership when one person has unrealistic
expectations either, constantly wanting you to read her mind
and fix all her negativity. No one can fix your life except you
and a good shrink. If you want to treat a man this way, don't be
surprised if he does not stick around. If you are an apostle of
negativity, then you need to find happiness. He cannot do this
for you.

If, however, you nurture your mate with support and acceptance, he may enjoy his partnership with you. Other women will then look less attractive to him. If you understand his needs and nurture him, not only will you have the faithful ring, but you will be the diamond in his heart.

It is also important to note that men need direction. I am not saying this in a condescending manner. I mean this literally. A man will move mountains to please the woman he loves, but she needs to tell him what pleases her. For example, a woman needs to tell a man what she wants for Christmas or what she wants him to do around the house. Be specific. Don't play games and punish him for not reading your mind. How is he going to know unless you tell him? Given that men are filled with testosterone and driven by hormones, it is a wise woman who tells him what pleases her in bed. A man hates an "ice queen" between the sheets. He craves stimulating, impulsive, wild love making. Therefore, a woman needs to tell her man what pleases her because he is simple minded. He likes information in concrete terms that he can understand. No head games. No manipulation. He likes open transparency and the freedom to talk openly and honestly without persecution.

In times of discord, tell your man what you want and avoid harping on what he did not do. Nagging, hounding, and complaining shuts him off like a burned out light bulb and makes him respect you less. Eventually, the relationship will erode and another woman may be waiting for him to arrive at her place while you are crying yourself to sleep in bed alone at night. With that said, put your ovulation thermometer away, keep your uterus in check and refrain from bringing life into a dead marriage.

The King's Honorable Palace

Thou shall believe that with all the strength
comprised within me, I shall speak the truth,
even if it is ever so painful

12

King Daddy

When we read the Cinderella story when we were young girls, we cheered for the poor girl who finally found her savor on the white horse. The truth, however, is that this is a fairytale. Most women who put themselves in dangerous situations (with men) have wanted the fairytale. However, they simply do not know what to look for in men. It is difficult to find a King when you have been romanticized by the vision of the handsome Prince. The reason for this is that many women have never had a decent father figure who helped them distinguish fantasy from reality. How can you find a good man or even identify the signs of a good man when you have no idea what to look for? When a woman has never had an honorable father, she becomes susceptible to the dishonorable Prince who will use and abuse her. Let us discuss this further.

Little girls have a grandiose vision of what a Daddy is. A Daddy can move mountains and stop trains with his humungous feet, all while grabbing the moon with the palm of his hand and delivering it right to her. He can move the motion in the ocean with his strength. The perfect Daddy can make everything right and defend her honor to anyone and anything. He is the Knight in shining armor that comes to her emotional rescue who is one-hundred feet tall and a million feet wide, and his love for her is boundless. She can wrap him around her little finger with the bat of an eye, and she can melt his heart with her tears when she cries. And this is because his love for her is boundless, timeless and will live on through infamy. She is soaked in his emotional security blanket and knows he is always there for her. He will never leave her. Her father teaches her that she is deserving of love from every source and that she is special, worthy and okay, even with imperfections.

This is the image the little girl has of her father, and then one day she grows up. The fantasy sheds and suddenly she sees her father as a human being, but his love for her remains. She recognizes his faults and accepts his imperfections. Her relationship with him has set the stage for her to have intimate relationships with other men, and she someday finds a husband who has similar qualities.

If she had an absent father or a father that was a poor role model, however, she misses out on the maturity phase and still lives in that fantasy state, forever longing for the Daddy that did not exist. She may sacrifice everything, in many cases, just to be that special little girl to a man who will absolutely adore her.

She will put up with abuse, abandonment and any other form of hurtful treatment, all because he showed her qualities that resembled the fantasy man. Unfortunately, she is ripe for the con artist to pretend to be what she wants him to be. She has no idea what to look for in a good man. Who is a good man? What does he look like? What does he act like? One thing that should not be a priority to her is what he sounds like.

The King Defined

The father-daughter relationship is the first relationship a girl has with a man, and this is extremely important because she may someday grow up to be the mother of a son. If she is a needy woman who chooses a bum or an unfaithful Prince, she becomes a miserable woman with unstable emotions. Not only does she choose a poor role model (in a father for her boys) but, if she is a miserable woman, she will be a miserable mother and will, inadvertently, create monsters in her sons. These are the future serial players and *bad boys* on barstools on the right side of the bar from whom we will tell our girls to stay away. Consequently, her sons will most likely grow up with a negative view of women. The cycle continues. She runs the risk of breeding little players someday who become dishonorable men that destroy the lives of other women. Need I say more?

Power

One of the most important qualities in a man, as far as most women are concerned, is power. Women love powerful, strong

men. This can be financial, physical, sexual or emotional
because most women love to be taken care of in some form or
another and a weak man simply cannot do it. Before we
proceed, we need to define power.

Power is synonymous with strength and brings with it a
sense of security, stability and *everything is going to be okay*
feeling. This is why Daddies are so important to little girls. As
we get older and mature into womanhood, our Daddies are no
longer handsome Princes to us, but rather good, honest men that
will always be there for us. When we shed our unrealistic
expectations of our "Daddies," we realize they are only human.
They cannot move mountains and stop trains, but they can do
something else: love us. This love is most powerful because it
determines our self worth, which determines all that we will
attract to us.

The UnNoble Prince Transformed

Please grant me the courage to look in the mirror and change

13

Hole Digger

If you want to build a house, you must first dig the hole and level the foundation. You have to clear the landscape to make room for a new horizon, which takes time, planning and commitment. This also applies to your personal life.

Too many older men reflect on their lives in disgust and regret, questioning why they did the "stupid things" they did in their younger years. They remember the women they used and hurt; they remember the wives and children they lost; they remember the jobs they could not keep or the bottles of booze that kept them catatonic to the painful reality of life. It is a sad existence that continually lives in a black hole of darkness, but everything in life happens for a reason. It does not matter what happened yesterday or who said what about you. What matters is how you live your life today.

Society has always been quick to judge and condemn, but the wise ones understand that everyone is in different stages of spiritual, mental, emotional and psychological growth. We make choices based on the knowledge and maturity we have at the time. We learn lessons and, hopefully, become wiser. This is what life is about. Most of us mature and learn to be honest with ourselves and others. This is the very reason older men reflect in regretful stupors. This is also why second and third marriages usually last, while the first ones dissolve. It may take a few times to learn lessons. The key is to build on the past as it levels the foundation for the future. Dig your foundation now by exploring what (in your past) has made you behave in destructive ways.

The Shining Mirror

If you have been a player, young or old, and have now come to terms with the undesired consequences that your behaviors have caused, you are the only one who can change your life. If you do not identify the causes and origins of your behaviors, you are destined to repeat them and will continue to create more destruction.

The next step is to understand that change is a long, difficult process that takes commitment and, in most cases, professional help. When I say professional help, I do not mean three trips to the "crazy couch." I mean two-to-three years of weekly visits to a trained psychologist who can assist you in making lifestyle changes. You need trained professionals to hold you accountable and keep you on track. He or she will help you accept your fears and challenges and will help you with the process of change.

Change occurs slowly through transformation of the mind. We slowly learn to identify what we feel. We begin to understand that our actions or reactions derive from our feelings, which come from our perceptions. Thus, our thoughts (perceptions) create feelings, and our feelings drive us to react. Players, for example, commonly react from fear of commitment. They run from conflict (uncomfortable situations) and may constantly strive for instant gratification, jumping from one woman to another, hoping to find relief from the last one. Remember the pillars? It is now time to destroy the pillars so that you can learn the art of intimacy.

Action Plan

Before you drive from California to New York, you have to map your route so you know where you are going. You have to plan the trip. The same is true for life. If we want to build that house we talked about, it makes no sense to jump right in without preparation and planning. Before you build a house, you must have a blue print. You have to know what you are going to build and what you want to accomplish.

If you decide to change, you have to start from the inside out, which requires an action plan. Please know, too, that rarely can people do it alone. Self help books do not work too well because we desperately need the support and guidance to do the hard work required. Too often we lie to ourselves or cannot recognize our destructive patterns of thinking and acting. Professionals force us out of denial by showing us our deficits and strengths. They help us tear down our "inner" shacks so that we can build new houses. Most importantly, we need trained professionals to help us with the necessary skills to help us change. This is called behavior modification, which is very useful to those who have had so many years of unhealthy behaviors that it seems impossible to change. Only a trained professional is able to help you work through the trauma from your dysfunctional childhood. Let us explore this point.

When we are small children, we learn who we are by the way our caregivers treat us. We were trained to think of ourselves as our caregivers had done. Therefore, if we were trained to have negative thoughts about ourselves, then we have negative feelings about who we are. When we feel negative, we tend to react negatively to situations that hurt us and we may take out our frustrations on those around us. The problem with this is that we do not react on a conscious level. It just happens, like the way we breathe air to survive. Unfortunately, once we react, we suffer the consequences. As discussed earlier, negativity consists of heavy energy that can be harmful to your personal growth. Negativity is not exclusive to the sad woman hunched in the corner with a frown upon her face. It comes in many faces, forms and disguises, and the worst is when it hides behind a smile.

Wall Builders

When you buy a piece of land and clear the way to build a house, you need a "level" foundation to start your project. Once you lay the foundation, you can build from the ground up. You have to clear away the undesirable to make way for the new. Once you build the foundation, you build the beams and wall structures. The purpose for the walls is to section off spaces for privacy inside the home. After some hard work and a length of time, you have a new home. This concept is also applied to intimate relationships.

An honorable man uses blue prints that were carefully planned. He made the investment with the intent on following through with the commitment and then puts forth the time, money and energy to build the home. Once the decision was made, he followed through. He then enjoys his house and, with more carefully planning, he finds a compatible mate to join him in making a home. He uses the walls in his house as a measure to "give" and "take" privacy for which the walls were intended.

A dishonorable man, the player, however, uses the walls to keep others out. In terms of relationships, a dishonorable man does not carefully plan his blueprint for his home. He does not clear the foundation very well. His past "baggage" invades his world when the *half-assed* home is built. In relationships, this man builds several walls in his life, pillars as we noted earlier, which make it almost impossible for anyone to get too close to him.

Unlike the honorable King, these men may be characterized as commitment phobic players who dream steadily of the perfect fantasies that never arrive. They are not dependable because their desires may change, depending on what room of the house they are in at the moment. This is what makes them so hurtful.

This problem infects his life and the life of every woman who is unsuspecting enough to become emotionally involved with him. Since there is no real cure for a commitment phobic, all this man can hope for is the courage and strength to reflect on his life and "clean out" all the painful baggage that has made him such an *asshole* to begin with, as many women would claim.

If you are a wall builder who keeps women out of your personal space, then your only hope of finding inner happiness is to explore what it is in your memory bank that has made you so terrified of intimacy. This takes time, energy and courage. It takes dedication and commitment. If I am talking to you, then you may want to think about this and cut loose the women you are dangling behind you. The beams and walls that are built on unsecured foundations will eventually end up collapsing in their own time.

Boys Don't Cry

When I was a child, I heard my father tell my brother not to cry like a "sissy girl." Consequently, my brother was afraid to cry. Sadly, he shoved his feelings below and the tears came flooding from him in every destructive way imaginable. He cried his whole life, only no one saw the tears.

The one point I want to make is that it takes courage to cry, but it takes more courage to take risks and stand up for the right thing at the risk of making others cry. Players are pleasers who need adulation from others, even at the risk of their own honor and integrity. Most players are still small boys fearing failure and disapproval. If they make any type of long-term commitment, it may be the "wrong" choice and then they feel compelled to run away again; consequently, they may be plagued by terrible cases of claustrophobia. If you are a player and have spent years in unstable situations, you may want to think about this. Do you tell others what they want to hear to gain approval or acceptance? Do you give in to others so that you can keep the peace? If so, you are not acting in your own best interest or in the best interest of others.

If you think of the consequences and rewards of your behaviors ahead of time, you will do the right thing most of the time. The key is to consider the ramifications to others beforehand. If you have a one-night-stand with Sally down the street, for example, and she becomes pregnant, what will happen? Do you ask (ahead of time) if you love Sally enough to spend the rest of your life with her? Can you imagine being in a situation where Sally is the only naked woman you will ever see again? That is what marriage is-- a life-long commitment. If you use a condom and it breaks, what happens? Is Sally stuck on you so much that she would purposely try to get pregnant with your child? Do you know her well enough to assess her stability? Would she want to force you to be attached to her in some way for the rest of your lives, either by marriage or child or both? How will Sally feel if you just *screw* her and walk out the door? Most importantly, how will it affect the unborn child? Would this child be conceived out of spiritual, compatible love with a best friend, the woman with whom you desire to partner in this life, as we discussed at the beginning of our conversation? Those are painful questions to which honorable men already know the answers. Players dive right in without considering any of these points.

Honorable men think about what they do. They make decisions based on more than just self-serving interests at the moment. If you want to have a one night stand, it is most honorable to be truthful to her from the beginning. You should also use protection. If this situation is agreeable to both of you, then you did the right thing.

Honorable men do not make life-long commitments based on mere obligation. They think long and hard before they choose a mate for life. If you are with a woman you do not truly love, someone you do not see as a compatible mate, then you are acting dishonorably if you keep her on a string for two years. It is even more dishonorable if you use her for "good" sex and then marry her out of obligation should she plan a pregnancy (after waiting two years for you to pop the question that has to do with *forever*). In the long term, this hurts her, the child, and possible future children. It will also hurt all the future women with whom you will fool around while you are "trapped" with her in a loveless marriage. You must remember that you are responsible for the choices that will end up hurting others. She will be hurt if you break it off with her, yes, and you may miss her terribly because she has become a habit to your life, but honorable men think beyond the discomfort of the present situation, and they do the right thing.

Honorable men choose partners who enhance their *being* on all levels. They choose partners that have the same goals, desires, and interests. They choose women who think like they think. These are the men that swing back and forth with their wives on the front porch when they are eight-five years old. This is the man in the movie *The Notebook* who stood by his wife until death, not out of mere obligation, but out of pure desire and devotion. I believe *commitment* is the operative word, a word that may terrify you.

Planting Seeds

I once heard a man say that he would not plant his seed where he would not want it to grow. This was a profound and honorable statement. He was aware that sexual intercourse with a woman may result in a new life creation, and his sperm is the seed. Too many dishonorable men overlook this fact when their dicks get hard. When I was a teenager, my father, in his unsophisticated attempt at giving me the man's perspective on the *birds and the bees*, blurted out to me crudely that *a stiff dick has no conscience*. He was right if we think about all the dishonorable players out there that love to get laid. Most players, however, lack responsibility. They worry about the consequences *after the fun has been had*.

If I am talking to you, here is a tip for your little black book (the secret) that women do not want you to know. Just as you will lie and scheme to get a woman in bed, she may lie and scheme to get you to the alter. Women are acutely aware of their reproductive cycles, and the manipulative woman knows she is most fertile in the middle of her cycle. If she is with a "noncommittal" man and has waited "long enough" for him to pop the question, she may just get him hot and hard during that time of the month, a time most convenient in the absence of a condom. The next month she cries *baby in the belly* with nowhere to turn, as one man voiced it. I have seen this happen many times. The player then finds himself in a world of confusion because now he is forced to make a decision, something he avoids at all costs. If he is worried about his reputation and how others will view him, as most dishonorable men do, then he may take the plunge. He sets himself up for a lifetime of pain.

Shortly after the alter, he may inevitably find a mistress or two or three and it keeps going. He is a wrecking ball in high gear. This is the consequence of dishonest, irresponsible behavior. Who gets harmed the worst? The kids.

With all this being said, you may want to think about where you plant your seed. I am going to talk very "frank" to you now in a language that many players understand. Ladies, please pardon my diction that I will use for emphasis.

You may want to think twice before lingering in a dead relationship for your own selfish reasons or for your cowardice refusal to face the discomfort of separating from a "good habit." Habits are not love. Sex is not love. A good "blow job" is not love. Good "pussy" does not stay good if everything else is missing. Therefore, you may want to think twice about leading on a woman with whom you have no long-term vested interest. Let her move on to find someone who does want to buy her goods. Be aware that commitment phobic men rarely end anything, just like they never officially start anything. They are always lingering on the sidelines building comfortable pillars (pretending they are in or out), because they hate to make definite decisions. If you make a decision, then (in most cases) this means you make a commitment to something. If you are honest with yourself, you will admit that deep in your heart you really long for a loving relationship, not interactions that have kept you trapped in your own pillars all these years. Now is the time for change. It is up to you.

The Hanged Man

An honorable man does not stay stuck in a loveless marriage for years because he "knocked up" a long-term girlfriend that he was just *not that into* marrying. If a man does not feel the drive to commit to a woman for more than a year or two, there is a reason. Think about this for a second. If you are searching for the right land to build a home, you seek a real estate agent and visit the sites. If you want the land, you know it. You buy it. If you do not want the land, you know it, and you do not keep going back to visit the same piece of property that holds no value to you. If a man wants to buy a car, he goes to a dealer, prices it and buys it. He does not keep returning to test drive a car he does not want. Time is of the essence for men, and honorable ones do not waste time and energy on that which they have no investment.

Choosing a partner for life is not like buying a wrench from the hardware store. You can always return the wrench and forget about it, but it may be more complicated to "get rid of" a bad relationship. If you don't choose the right partner, you could be in for a lifetime of pain, especially if you put yourself in a situation where you are trapped. The key is to find the right woman, but you have to know what you are looking for. A man will usually choose a woman much like his mother or the direct opposite of his mother. Of course there are exceptions, but I have seen this to be the case most of the time.

With all that being said, what kind of woman are you looking for? Make a list of qualities that you want in a woman, and I am not talking about physical features. A pretty face and big boobs get ugly after a while if you are fighting all the time. If you don't know exactly what you want in a woman, then at least write down what you don't want in her. I recently heard a news story that made my head turn twice. A woman from a Central American country called in a bomb threat to an airport hoping the threat would ground the airplanes, prohibiting her boyfriend from taking his journey. To make matters worse, the man was on his way to an important work event for his career. When she was busted, she claimed she missed him too much and did not want him to leave her. Now, if a woman ever calls in a bomb to an airport to hold you back, you may want to run out the door without even opening it. This is one manipulative and disturbed young lady and may cause you a lifetime of pain. As I have said to the ladies, the choice, of course, is yours.

When it comes to marriage, an honorable man usually knows what he wants, even while battling the natural urge to hold onto his autonomy. Remember that an honorable man manipulates situations (not people). If he thinks she is the one for him, he will do it in such a way that nudges her to coax him into marriage. Once he realizes it is safe to give up his autonomy to her, he will then trust her enough to "settle" him.

There once was a study conducted that asked numerous couples across the globe who initiated marriage, the man or woman. In almost all the cases the men said they never would have gotten married had it not been for the wives. I do not believe this is because men do not want to get married. I contend it is because a man needs to be coaxed to succumb to the love of a good woman, the woman he deems "suitable" or a proper match.

In most cases, an honorable man does not put himself in life-long commitments unless he is sure he wants to buy the goods. He will not (likely) flirt with the danger of getting trapped. If by chance he marries and for reasons beyond his control the marriage turns out to be too unbearable, he may take action to either fix the marriage or divorce. This man most probably will not continue to have more children in an impossible situation, like many players do. He realizes that this choice will ultimately create generations of pain and turmoil, and he may ultimately fall from Grace and run around on her anyway. Therefore, an honorable man is rarely in this predicament because he is willing to go through the pain of separation from a long-time girlfriend with whom he saw no future or is strong enough to end a marriage that has been dead for years. Even a highly religious man, if he is truly honorable, may realize that God would grant forgiveness for a divorce if the ends justified the means.

My entire theme to everything in this book is truth. I am not condoning divorce or suggesting separation. I am imploring men to be honest and to finally stop living the lies that I (we) see all the time. Every month there appears to be a high profile figure in the news who is busted with affairs, love children, internet texting affairs, porno rings, playgirls, prostitutes, and need I continue? How do you think the wives, children, family members and, yes, even mistresses feel when these guys are busted? These women have to pick themselves up from rock bottom after being emotionally destroyed. If I am talking to you and you are guilty of this type of destruction, then you have some soul searching to do.

The Deed

Once you build your house, you have completed your mission. The deed is yours. If you have a strong house built to city and state regulations and guidelines, you can now focus on the cosmetics of the house. Just as we had a one-on-one conversation before with the women folk in this audience, now let us have a little chat. Take out your writing tablet and make an inventory list that helps you understand yourself a little better. Use the left side of the page to write down a list of all the adjectives or things that would describe your father or male role model. What kind of man was he? Use the right side to list the kind of man that the women in your life have told you that you are. How do they view you? Do you see any similarities? Turn over the paper and list all that will describe how your father treated your mother. If it hurts while you are writing, do not close this book and walk away. Everything will just follow you. Feel it and let the feelings keep coming. If you need to cry, then cry. You are alone. No one will see. On the right side of the page, list the characteristics of your mother. Was she strong or weak? How did your father make her feel? How did she make you feel as a result of her own feelings? This is not a professional inventory; it is a rough draft to get you started. Are there any similarities between your childhood and adulthood? Your therapist or psychologist can help you with the rest.

The only one who can change your life is you. I firmly believe anyone can change with the will, desire and resources to do so. Now is your time to transform and become the honorable King you admire in other men.

The Dadfather

I once knew an old man that had a green thumb with the living things planted in the earth. He loved to plant flowers and nurture life. The only problem is that he would end up with dead stuff all over the yard because he never stuck to anything. He promised himself every time that he was going to start a beautiful garden and keep it going, but it never happened. He would get bored and stop nurturing it all. He had no long-term commitment to the life he created. Consequently, everything died. The old man decided that he would stop promising himself he would do something that he was not disciplined enough to do. Therefore, he bought fake flowers for the porch and installed rock instead of shrubbery for landscaping purposes.

If players had a similar mind set when it comes to fatherhood, there would be a lot less pain in the world and the jails would be empty. It is surprising that players, who jump from one woman to the next and from one thing to the next, want to be fathers at all. However, the majority of players love kids and make it a goal to "leave their legacy" behind by having kids. Once they hit their mid thirties, many will marry just to have kids. The problem with this scenario is that they rarely understand the fundamental differences between being a father and a dad.

Any male can "father" a child by ejaculating sperm into a woman. However, once life is created, it has to be forever nurtured. It takes a lot of hard work, serious commitment and dedication. A father is more than sperm that creates life before abandoning the woman, leaving her to raise the child by herself. You can visit any prison and ask the prisoners what a father ought *not* to be.

A dad, however, is a father with everything else added to it. I will call him the *dadfather* because, not only does his sperm create life, but his life is spent creating a human being. In order for the dad to be the kind of man a child needs, he must be willing to give up who he is for the rest of his life. This is a choice that needs to be carefully planned, and not all men can live up to the challenge, just like the old man with the "temporary" green thumb.

If you are a player who lives life for pleasure and seeks to meet your own needs, then you may want to think about having kids. Perhaps you are not cut out to be a dadfather, and that is okay. The key is to know this beforehand. If you know you are not cut from *dadfather cloth* and you proceed to have children anyway, then this is irresponsible behavior. You will most likely end up abandoning your kids in one way or another. This is not fair to them. You decide where you plant your seed and whether or not you want your seed to grow.

Let us discuss what it takes to be a real dad: You must go to baseball games, soccer games, Birthday parties and other kid functions after a long, hard day's work. You have to give up all that you loved to do — all that once filled your time slots to these new "obligations," as some would say. It also requires hours of homework, after a long hard day's work. It requires running to the emergency room in the middle of the night, right before a long, hard day's work. It requires setting boundaries, limits and expectations and dealing with frustrations when the child does not listen. It requires teaching and learning. It demands ardent listening skills that can test your patience. When life stressors mount and the bills add up and your marriage goes sour, you will want to pack it in. You want to throw your hands in the air and scream.

Realistically speaking, your whole life is consumed with another human being. If you have always been a self-absorbed man who was trying to get your needs met or searching for something you never found, then you are going to be in direct conflict with your child because kids are, by nature, totally self absorbed, too. Their needs should and must come before yours. If you can't handle this, then you may want to reconsider fatherhood. Kids can't comprehend the corporate time schedule and the mere fact that Daddy has needs. A five- year old child, for example, does not understand that Corporate Boss Ernest arrived and needs you to do a week of sixteen hour days. All he knows is that Dad is never around. Consequently, you are unintentionally abandoning your child.

If you love money and "things" and you do not have a plush job that allows you to live the way you "dream," then you need to think twice before having kids. You will have diapers, food, clothes, medical bills, orthodontic bills, school supply bills, entertainment bills, huge Christmas gift bills, Birthday tabs, and don't forget that college education and automobile. Are you willing to sacrifice all that you have and all that you are for the sake of another human life that you can't return, once out of the womb? A child is nonreturnable.

If you strive to "produce" and climb the corporate ladder, you need to think twice before marrying a woman who needs a

9-5 husband and demands that you to take care of her emotional needs.

You must know what you are capable of before making a commitment that you can't keep. If you marry out of obligation and proceed to have children, you will most likely neglect your wife's needs and the needs of your children. Frustrations will mount. Fights will begin. Tensions will linger. Distance will pull your marriage apart. Needs will go unmet. I will get more in depth with my scenario: You will stray to another woman. Your wife will become unhappy and unstable. She may take it out on the kids. Your son will throw down his toy truck in a fit of tantrum rage and tell you he hates you. You chase after him as he hides under his bed, bating you to climb under there after him. You scream to your wife to get control of him, and she screams at you that you are a piss-poor father because you are never home. The phone rings and it is Corporate Ernest, telling you to be there an hour early tomorrow morning, and then your wife screams some more because you are never home. The tensions continue to mount. You get a call from your son's teacher saying he kicked another four-year old in the balls, and then your daughter's seventh-grade teacher sends you an email claiming that your daughter got into a huge cat fight at lunch, busting some girl's jaw. You want to get on an airplane and never return. You want to walk away and not deal with any of it. You want out! But then you remember how your father took off and left you, your mother and your three brothers without a penny. You remember how your mother used to scream to your father that he was a piss-poor husband and father because he was never there. Then one day he disappeared. You can't stand the son of a bitch because he was never there, but you can't think about that right now because Ernest is waiting patiently in the tech lounge. The meeting was supposed to be held twenty minutes ago. You get through the week and then the month, but what about next month? Am I making sense yet?

Therefore, know your limitations and accept who you are as a man. There is nothing wrong with deciding *not* to have children. It is wrong, however, to become a father while knowing you do not have the ability to be a dad. It is called responsibility. Children desperately need it.

In closing, go forward with the acceptance of who you are as a man. If you can't do it, then don't do it. Just be open and honest with the woman you are with and find a woman who, as we discussed several times in this book, has the same goals, passions and dreams as you. You may need a woman who, also, wants to climb the corporate ladder and who does not want the responsibility of bringing life into this world. The choice, as always, is yours.

The Prince's Red Flags

Look again! The Prince's nose just grew two inches while you weren't looking!

14

I Am Not Crazy and I Certainly Am No Fool!

Given enough time in your situation, you will finally come to a cross road where you will be forced to make changes. When people have had enough, they either explode or implode, and disasters force change either way. You do not want to go down the self-destructive path like stalking him or doing anything resentful that will come back to haunt you in the end. He is not worth it, and it will put you in a far worse predicament than you are right now.

Betrayal of any kind is bitter, but when you have so much invested in someone and they blatantly deceive you, your world comes crashing down. If I am talking to you, then you probably cannot escape thoughts, memories, questions, and suspicions that haunt you. Doubt keeps entering your mind. Every time you turn around, something does not seem right. You believe that if you only had the truth, you could find peace. It is like the woman who knows for years she has a physical ailment but has no concrete evidence and then one day years later, the doctors tell her she has cancer. Although this woman is devastated, she now has relief because at least she knows what she is fighting. The questions have been answered and the acceptance process can begin.

One of the most common concerns women have is how do I know if I am the crazy one or if he really is being unfaithful? How can I tell a red flag from a white flag? Most importantly, what do I do when I see some of the signs, but I have no proof? The answer is simple: Watch his behavior and listen to what you see. Here are some testimonials that are based on situations I have seen.

The Passive Terrorist
Princess Grace

Grace was dating a married man, Brent, for two years. It took her a while to get involved with him because she did not want to become involved with a married man. Brent, however, ardently pursued Grace until she succumbed to his advances. Brent had felt that, finally, after all these years he had met his soul mate. He was crazy about her and became emotionally dependent on her.

After some time, Grace found herself in a problematic situation because she was falling in love with him. They had tumultuous arguments because she could not stand his vacillation and deceptions. It was like a roller coaster ride: he was connected to her and then would disappear for days. She ended it numerous times, but he would crawl back and beg her not to leave him. No matter what, he could not stay away from her for very long and knew just how to manipulate her to draw her back into his world.

Brent told Grace that he could not stand to be with his wife, but he could not bare to leave his children. He also told her that his wife did not love him and was only in the marriage for a "meal ticket," as he called it. He also said his wife was emotionally cold and somewhat abusive to the kids. If this were the case, Grace understood why he was having an affair and felt bad for his predicament.

Two years into their relationship, Brent was with Grace at her home, where they had planned to spend the day together, but his wife, Karen, left a frantic message that sent him packing in a tailspin. She had called his work and was told that he was not in today. She was furious, threatening to come to his work "right now" to find out where he is. Brent was a nervous wreck and left in a hurry.

Grace was angry because he jumped when his wife "pulled the strings," as she claimed. "If things are so bad as you say, then you need to tell her the truth and stop jerking me around, dropping me at the top of the hat every time she gets upset," Grace told him. She was turned off by his lack of courage to deal with conflict. He avoided it at all costs and, on numerous occasions throughout their affair, Brent would jump to his wife's demands. This left Grace feeling worthless and unimportant.

As the story continues, Brent left Grace's house in a frenzy, apologizing to her, promising to get together the next day. "I will work something out, Grace, I promise! I am so sorry and this will not always be like this. Please believe me. I will make the change, just give me some time!"

The next day came and Brent did not call. He emailed her at the last minute saying his son was ill, and they needed to take him to the doctor. He rescheduled with her for Tuesday and promised to call her Monday morning. When Monday morning arrived, he did not call. He emailed her to tell her his phone went dead, and he needed a new battery. When Tuesday arrived, he emailed her and told her that he was sorry, but he could not make it today because he had been called to a Supervisor's Board Meeting and his phone was still dead. Would it be okay to get together Thursday? Grace was angry, but agreed. When Thursday came, Brent emailed her to say that he had come down with the flu and would be out the rest of the week. "I am so sorry, Grace, please forgive me!" He had yet to phone her.

Clearly he was giving Grace the run around. He was avoiding her and giving her the *heave ho*. Grace then wrote him a scathing email, feeling like she had been taken for a ride. Something was not right. She had so many pent up emotions she could hardly stand it.   She did not know if he had another woman or if something terrible happened in his home. She never thought it was Karen because he repeatedly said he had no connection with his wife and that he was only with her for the kids.

Brent responded with anger claiming that Grace did not care how he was and that she was insensitive to his well being. Grace damn near threw plates at the wall in rage because he negated with disregard his numerous exits on her. He was jerking her around.

Weeks passed. When they finally talked, Brent said he was angry because the last time he was with her she demanded he leave his kids. "How insensitive are you that you expect me to abandon my kids?" He asked her.

Brent had deliberately abandoned Grace repeatedly because he was angry that she gave him a semi-ultimatum, only he did not tell her this. He could not express his anger to her; yet, he did the very thing that he knew would hurt her the most. This man strung her along with dead promises and left her hanging without answers, which was quite contrary to the way he behaved when he pursued her at the beginning of their affair. It was at this point that Grace finally knew what she had gotten herself into. She realized just how disturbed this man really was. Brent was obviously passive aggressive because he knew that abandoning Grace would hurt her the worst, and it would teach her a lesson about expecting anything more from him. This made her angry, which gave him an excuse to blame her for their conflict.

The truth is that he did not want to leave his wife. The conflict that Brent created put the blame on Grace, but it also gave him time away from her to put his marriage back in line. This cruel, manipulative, and deceptive game could have dangerous consequences. When I say getting involved with a married man can ruin your life, it is this emotional roller coaster road to which I am referring. This kind of man is a ticking bomb that will blow up your emotions at any moment. He always has an agenda, and his wife and kids will come first.

He felt Grace was getting too close and the thought of leaving his kids was too much. He pushed her back in a safe comfort zone. He could not distinguish between "abandoning his kids" and divorcing his wife because, to him, they were the same thing. He could not see that divorcing his wife and exiting a bad marriage would ultimately save his relationship with his kids, as long as he kept them close to his heart and tended to their needs.

Grace was devastated because he used her weaknesses against her. This type of player is very dangerous because he knows your weaknesses and will use them to his advantage when need be. If you pressure him, as Grace did, he will employ passive aggressiveness in an attempt to get even with you for pressuring him. It is dangerous because he will slowly torture you emotionally by doing the very thing that will hurt you the worst, as Brent did Grace, until you break and react negatively. When you explode, everything will become your fault because this man does not take responsibility for his actions.

This kind of behavior is dangerous on all levels and may drive some women to do crazy things from emotional imbalance. This is when the mistress storms to his front door confessing all to the wife, or when she pulls out a gun and shoots him. When women realize they are being had like this, they may become imbalanced, especially when there is a strong emotional investment.

The key is to get away from this type of man. If you are a mistress involved with a passive aggressive player that always has his own agenda and uses various excuses to continue his game playing, distance yourself emotionally and physically. He will not change. Know in your heart that he has serious problems and that no matter who he is with, he will hurt them. Pity his poor wife.

If you are a wife married to a passive aggressive player that you can't seem to locate, you may want to plan your way out of the marriage. You need not ask him any questions or look to him to convince you that you are wrong. Chances are you are dead right when you know he is up to something. People with passive aggressive behaviors are not honorable and are master manipulators. Further, passive aggressiveness is the worst form of abuse because it is impossible to defend against. He is not worth it. If you have children and are dependent on him financially, then you may want to distance yourself emotionally and plan your way out. Play his game. Deceive him the way he is deceiving you. Take care of yourself and your children. Plan an exit and keep on going. There are many honorable men out there who will not hurt you with passive aggressive deceit, a good man who will treat you with dignity and respect.

The Time Dancer
Queen Kelly

Kelly was married to Paul for five years. Outward appearances portrayed Paul as a faithful husband, good provider and loving father. He went to church on Sundays and was held in high esteem. Paul's life with Kelly seemed stable and routine. He loved her but never fell "in love" with her. He felt guilty because he knew he was distant on the intimate level and did whatever he could to deny his *lack of love*.

He managed to maintain an affair on the side through manipulation and storytelling. One time during the hot summer months he wanted to spend time with Mistress Kim. He called his wife on his way home to tell her about this terrible fire that was currently roaring through the neighborhoods and hills. He described the fire in great detail and then railed against the inconvenience of traffic. He pontificated that it was a terrible fire and many people lost their homes and lives. Yes, this was true. The only problem with the story is that it happened ten hours earlier on the other side of town. It was convenient because the commotion of the fire was still occurring, and all accounts could be verified. His wife was so engaged in the details of the fire that she lost sight of the real fire that was happening in Kim's bedroom.

Another time during the Christmas season, Paul wanted to spend some time with his mistress and used events at work as an excuse. He had to put together a large staff party with all the heads of service in the lower firms of the corporation. The responsibility was overwhelming. Paul would coordinate the events and compress an agenda for the speakers who were being honored. He also had to organize the food services and devise a time schedule, which was what he was particularly gifted at doing. He informed Kelly of all the details and spoke proudly of his accomplishments. Kelly was impressed and so engaged in the details that she missed the very thing he wanted her to overlook. Yes, it was a spectacular event and Paul did a fantastic job. The only problem with this story is that the party happened the previous Friday.

Paul is a classic example of a time dancer. This type of deception is detected when you step back and look at the entire character of the man. A reliable, honorable man does not commit this hurtful deception. This type of emotional fraud can be easily detected if you realize that his daily pattern of behavior is not honest. He may use the same tactics with different people in his life. For example, he may have a commitment to the neighbor with which he does not follow through or may also use deceptive tactics that will buy him some time to procrastinate with other obligations, all while trying to keep face.

Keep in mind that a phony cannot compartmentalize phoniness. Unfortunately (for him) this is one thing that won't stay in the pillar. The key is to know your mate's mode of operation when dealing with other people. Watch him in action. Listen to the values he employs. Does he lie about small things? Does he generate excuses that make people feel stupid should they reject what he is saying? I once knew someone that went on and on about a death in the family, which was an excuse to get out of an obligation. Should anyone dare question this type of excuse, he or she would look like an idiot. This type of man generates tumultuous excuses to ensure success in his agenda. Honorable men do not behave in deceptive ways.

If you are a mistress who sits back and watches a player lie like this, you may want to boot his ass out the door before he does the same things to you. It is mode of operation.

If you are a wife in this situation, you may ask yourself if you want to spend time and energy checking every story he tells before investing in what he is saying. If he provides too many details and carries on like a runaway motor mouth, he is probably orchestrating a lie. The more he digs in a hole, the deeper the hole gets and the more visible it becomes. Pay attention. You have to decide if you really want to exert the energy investigating everything he says. It is draining and will attract negative energy to you. Eventually you will be consumed with hatred and disdain for him.

The Distractor
Queen Mary

Mary and Ralph were married for ten years and had two children together. Mary noticed that Ralph was happy-go-lucky right before he went on his monthly conferences, but upon his return became distant and "dopy," as she would call it. She was suspicious that he had someone on the side and asked him point blank to confirm or deny her fears. He put his arms around her and assured her that he had so much pressure in his life with work and three kids and a wife that he barely had time to breath. "Where would I ever find the time to have a fling?" He asked her. Although he was convincing, Mary was still suspicious. Ralph then suggested she join him at the next conference that just so happened to be near her mother's house a few hours away. Mary was now sure that she was just imagining these "crazy thoughts" because he never would have suggested off the cuff that she join him had he been guilty of messing around on her.

Once at the hotel, Ralph shuffled to the crowd as they gathered together in the lobby. About ten minutes later, he returned to Mary and said his boss, Hank, had suggested an "all nighter" in the Ballroom Conference Center on the lower level of the hotel. "It would probably be best if you spent tonight with your mother, Mary, and then we can spend tomorrow night together. We have too much work tonight, and I want to get it all out of the way now so we can have some time together away from the kids. What do you think?" Mary was agreeable and all suspicions had been admonished. After all, the entire script played out right before her eyes.

What Mary did not know was that the conference did not start until the following day. Ralph had planned in advance to meet his mistress on the first night and knew that everyone would meet beforehand to decide where the conference would be held on the following day.

This is a dishonorable distracter who had everything planned and organized in advance. He distracted his wife in a manipulative, coy manner that was as believable as watching an *A list* actor perform his script. This is a dangerous man because it is impossible to detect the truth. He can retort with any "line" at the spur of the moment. He is always prepared and forearmed with some plot to hide the truth. You almost have to assume that everything is a lie with this type of character.

If you are a suspicious wife, as was Mary, you may want to think twice before approaching him. Do not let on that you are suspicious because he will distract you and distort all the facts to his advantage. If you are honest to yourself, you will admit that you need him to tell you that you are wrong. If you see all the signs that something is not right, then you are probably correct. Do not doubt yourself. Allow yourself to feel the painful truth that is staring you right in the face. Do you want him to convince you that you cannot trust your own judgment? If this is the case, then you are asking him to convince you that you are crazy.

You have to grieve (for the loss of him) while you are still with him, which is a difficult task to do. You must gather the strength and start planning your future without letting on that you know the truth. Your best bet is to gather proof before you approach him. This man is a smooth operator and can talk his way out of a paper bag if you give him the opportunity. Do you want to stay with a man who plays you like a Chess game and holds you in low esteem? Do you want to stay with a man who runs around with other women and then treats you in such a demeaning manner? Think about this.

If you are a mistress who has watched this man play games and hurt his wife to this degree, you may want to think about what you are doing with him. If he dishonors his wife, he will surely dishonor you someday. He obviously has a psychological problem because, if he is such a good liar who shows no remorse or guilt, he may be pathological. How can you trust him? Do you think he will be faithful to you? The choice, as always, is yours.

The Cool Aid Giver
Queen Vicky

Vicky and Allen were married for twenty-three years and had five lovely children. By all appearances they lived a happy life together. What Vicky found out after years of marriage was that Allen had numerous long-term affairs, one that started before their marriage began.

Vicky was devastated when she was forced to face reality. The five children, however, were not surprised. All the signs were transparent, but Vicky would confess now, in retrospect, that she looked the other way. She needed him to tell her lies so that she could continue to keep face and remain in the marriage.

Throughout their marriage, Allen's behaviors were transparent. He hid clothes in his trunk. When Vicky asked about them, he told her they were work clothes to be taken to the cleaners. "Why would I stick them in a hamper only to take them to the cleaners the next day? Why not just stick them right in the trunk, Vicky?" He would ask. Further, Allen had one away conference a month and weekly night conferences that went very late, but this pattern would last for six months and then suddenly stop. Vicky wondered why conference schedules were so erratic. "It is sort of like taking a college course, Vicky. They begin and then end. Another one starts up," he told her. The problem with this is that Allen's coworker, John, never went to conferences. In addition, the telephone would ring (before the cell phone days) at the same time a day, but the caller hung up when Vicky answered. Allen then mysteriously left the house (after the hang up) for cigarettes or food items that he had no intention of eating. This pattern, too, would only last about six months. To add insult to injury, Allen would shift in and out of moods during the six months and, toward the end of the six months, he would become depressed. The following months, however, filled Allen with joy. To make matters worse (upon the internet days), Allen had a secret password on his email account. When Vicky asked why it was so secret, he told her that he needed privacy in case anyone from his job tried to hack into his computer. Add that to the locked cell phone in his pocket, and Vicky really became suspicious. When Vicky tried to answer it, he would grab it from her and tell her not to act like his mother. "My mother went through all my things as a kid, and I wish you would respect my privacy. If you can't trust me by now, then what do we have?" Vicky felt like he had punched her.

Allen had an answer for everything. Although Vicky saw the signs, she could not grasp reality because Allen was very intimate with her and treated her as though they were best friends. "How could he be seeing another woman when we have the greatest love making?" Vicky was perplexed.

Allen kept his marriage together by feeding his wife the poisonous cool aid that continued to allow her to save face in a dead marriage. He cleverly intellectualized everything and minimized his wife's ability to create common sense in her mind. His behavior is sociopathic because he has the inability to feel the consequences (of his actions) to his wife or anyone else. The truth of the matter is that Allen wanted his cake, and he ate it too. This is indicative of a player who wants his stable, secure world with his wife, but also wants the fantasy romance with other women that keeps him on an emotional high. We may also assume he may have had a sexual addiction because, by all accounts, he was able to spread it all around with no problem.

Allen had no intention of leaving his wife, all while

meandering in and out of extra affairs with naïve women. In retrospect, his wife could tell by his moods when he was entering into a new affair and when he had just exited one.

This type of player has no idea what real intimacy is. In a real "relationship," nothing is locked. In a real "relationship," nothing is hidden from your best friend, your partner for life. You do not hide calls or change the screen on the computer when your partner enters the room. You do not pay the U.S. Post Office every month for a secret P.O. Box where secret mail is delivered to you. A marriage means that everything belongs to "us" because together we are one.

If you are married to this type of player, you must ask yourself if you are drinking the cool aid to keep your stability together. Then ask yourself to examine the loneliness and pain that you suppress so deep within you that you can no longer find it. Take inventory of how unstable your emotions have become because every time you know he is on the prowl, it is as though he sticks a knife in you. How can any wife continue to love a man who keeps stabbing her?

If you are a mistress going with a man who treats you like this, then you must realize that you are being treated like his other wife, and there very well may be two or three more of you waiting in the wind for his attention. Would you eventually like to graduate to "spouse status" with this man? Now is your time to run like hell.

The Orchestrator
Queen Kate

Kate was getting very suspicious of her husband, Larry, because he was acting distant and aloof. She asked him probing questions, but Larry, keenly aware of Kate's behaviors, was one step ahead of her. He did not want her to find out that he had a date with his mistress the following week, so he distracted her. He told her there was a huge problem at work and that his job may be in jeopardy. He also said that one of the guys suggested he seek legal counsel. Larry poured his heart out, seeking his wife's pity and advice because he knew that she would offer suggestions. "Go see an attorney," she instructed empathetically. Larry listened and then said, "Okay, I will see what I can do." By this time, Kate's defenses were down. She felt sorry for her husband and, at the same time, was relieved that he was finally confiding in her. She believed they were growing closer together, through his crisis.

The next day Kate called him at work making sure he was okay. She even made a special dinner for him because she assumed he was under a lot of stress. Larry called her later to tell her that he took her advice and had an appointment with the best attorney that was three hours away. The only appointment available was next Friday, which happened to be the heaviest traffic day. Kate was relieved that he was "bonding" with her. Her defenses were down.

Larry went off with his mistress for twelve hours that day. When he returned home, he told Kate that the attorney said there was nothing to worry. His legal problems were solved. He dismissed the events as though they never happened.

In this situation, Larry orchestrated premeditated deception. This is the most dangerous form of deception because he uses your emotions to confuse the truth. He *becomes* his lie, like an actor becomes his script, as he engages you in false drama. He praised Kate for her "smarts" and, again, made her feel one-hundred feet tall. He complimented her for using her brains to help him. He enabled her codependency and distracted her focus so that she was helping him, not concentrating on his infidelity. This is an example of a man that has no honor because, not only did he deliberately deceive his wife, but he set it up to generate his wife's worry and concern for their livelihood. He was a clever orchestrator who understood that women bond emotionally; he used this to his advantage. If she generated so much energy trying to help him, it would make all suspicions disappear.

Not only was he cheating and deceiving his wife with another woman, but he was humiliating her with emotional exhaustion and worry. In this case, Larry exhibits sociopathic tendencies because he showed no remorse, guilt nor shame. The only way to detect this type of behavior is to constantly watch the other hand.

It is very unfortunate to hear stories like this, but this type of man does very well exist. How do you know if you are dealing with a man as sick as this because, like an actor, he can fool even the savviest mind? If you were raised in a loving home with protective parents, you would have learned the skills that you need in this situation. Simply watch the way a man does his life, and he will tell you who he is. If he was too dismissive when he returned home from the "attorney" after all that worry for a week, then that was a warning flag. A major ordeal does not just disappear without further discussion. Also, if Larry is behaving this way, it is most likely his mode of operation that he uses when needed. Kate may find a pattern of her husband creating a crisis, seeking her advice and then, all of the sudden, the problem suddenly vanishes without further discussion. This is a clue. Kate can listen to what Larry says on one hand, but then watch what he does with the other.

While he distracts you with drama and chaos on one hand, look at his other hand to watch where he goes and what he does. In fact, it is the wise woman that can catch a man right in his tracks during this phase of his operation. She lets the right hand spin on and on, all the while hiring a private investigator to follow him during this phase of his operation.

This type of man is clearly dangerous and is not worth the door of which to boot him out. If you are the wife in this situation, you may want to ponder your future with this man. The choice is yours.

If you are the mistress in this situation, you may want to run as fast as you can away from this guy without looking back. If you eventually end up with him, what kind of stories will he tell you?

The Crazy Maker
Princess Connie

Connie was dating a married man, Fred, for three years. She noticed strange behaviors that she could not interpret. When she was with him, he adored her. His body language, touch, actions and words all indicated that he was very much in love with her, and he repeatedly told her that he wished they could be together permanently. In fact, he knew "deep in his gut" that someday they would be together. He confessed he felt guilty because of his kids and that he just couldn't stand being with his wife. He said there was no privacy in the house and that his wife constantly watched him and "picked at him."

Connie noticed a pattern: For two days after she was with him, he wrote her poetry and emails that were brimming with love. On the third day, however, something happened. He wrote her one line responses to her emails, which was contrary to his *prince-in-pursuit* ways. He then did not call her for days.

Fred fluctuated from hot to cold, leaving Connie to figure out what was happening. She became angry with him and wrote him a scathing email, which let him know how confused and hurt she was. He then responded with an angry email that minimized and negated everything she said. He scolded her for angry emotions. He told her he was offended by her angry tone and that he is always being watched on the computer. It was difficult with no privacy in the house. Connie was crushed. What happened? He was so distant and cold. He did not address any concerns.

She wrote him another email pouring out her confusion over his drastic change to which he did not respond. He had abandoned her, which tapped into her *childhood baggage* of abandonment.

A week passed. He finally wrote her an email saying he was sorry that he had not been in touch, but things were so hectic. Connie was perplexed because his email read like nothing negative had transpired between them. He said he missed and loved her without addressing anything from the previous week.

Once Connie was distant and cold, he was confused by her distance. Surprisingly enough, Connie eventually found out that he was jealous because he perceived that she was looking at other men.

Connie was dumb-founded and exhausted. She had recently written him several emails telling him that his behavior was making her pull away from him and she could not understand how he did not see the anger that his behavior had generated.

Fred obviously refused to address Connie's concerns. He distorted the facts by bringing "other men" into the equation, which took the spot light off of his behavior and deflected the concerns that Connie was trying to discuss.

If this story was difficult to follow, it is because Fred designed it this way. I shared the facts with you as they happened. This man is truly a crazy maker because he had Connie coming and going in various directions with very little information. His behavior is typical of a man who is guilt-ridden and confused about the two relationships he has in his life. On one hand, he loved Connie but, when he returns to his wife, felt tremendous guilt and began to bond again with his wife. He put Connie out of his mind and gave her the unconscious brush off, all while refusing to tell the truth. This man then blamed her, making her feel crazy, like poor Alice who must play peek-a-boo with the smell of women's cologne. He demonstrates selfish, impulsive behaviors that only meet his needs. Once Connie was gone for a while, however, he recruited her back into his pillar. He forced her into the role of pursuer. He puts her on the defensive, taking the spotlight off of the issue and places it on her. It is a very clever tactic that is a guaranteed *hate absorber*, as I coin it.

This man has narcissistic tendencies because he does not have the ability to feel the consequences to others. He lacks the courage to accept that he is not in love with his wife and, ultimately, ended up destroying Connie by swinging back and forth on the love tree.

This is typical of the married player who wants to come and go as he pleases. He is being dishonest to Connie by leading her on while bonding with his wife and children. If he was truly in love with his wife, he would not be with Connie. If he was truly in love with Connie, he would not be "loving" his wife. No one wins in this situation. If he is treating Connie this way, one may wonder how he treats his wife on a regular basis. It is no wonder he has marital problems. This type of man manipulates the woman's emotions with defensive (verbal) judo that makes her think she is crazy, all while infuriating her at the same time. He uses stonewalling and avoidance techniques to shut down the conversation. It is a red flag that he is hiding something.

If you are the wife in a situation like this where your husband is exhibiting major fluctuations towards you, this may be a sign that he has someone else. If he is loving one day and drastically critical the next, you may have a problem. If he is moody and distant, wanting you one minute and then condemning you the next for the smallest things, he may be comparing you to another woman. He sounds like an avoider and a punisher. You may want to think about taking an exit.

If you are the mistress in this situation, you may want to ask yourself if you want to someday be the wife married to a man that is fighting guilt for loving another woman.

The Backdraft Starter
Princess Melissa

Melissa was a naïve, childless widow who had spent several years alone after her husband died. She worked hard and continued her education, making a good career for herself. One day she met a charming man, Bill, who was married with four children. Melissa was confused because he was making advances towards her. Why would a "taken man" be interested in her? She refused his advances. Bill, however, continued to pursue her with gentleman charm. Melissa told Bill that they could be friends but nothing more.

Several days passed and Bill arrived at Melissa's house in a frantic state. He said that he could not take it anymore in his house with his wife. She was negative, bitter and always "picking" at him. She did not care about him as a man or as a person. His situation made him very lonely and distant towards his wife. She was harsh with the kids. He also said she had gained tons of weight, and he was turned off by her appearance. The sad story continued.

They had not had sex in years. In fact, he could not stand to be near her. Bill was disappointed that he had gotten "trapped' years ago when she became pregnant. "I was going to leave her at that time, and I started to distance myself from her to give her the hint that things were not good between us. Then we went on a preplanned trip and that was the night she got pregnant," Bill said. He continued by saying that he did not really love her and that is why he did not marry her until she was nine months pregnant. He felt it was his obligation.

Melissa listened to Bill's story and tried to help him figure out some type of solution. "Have you tried marriage counseling?" She asked. Bill rejected this notion because his wife would never do that. Bill dismissed all Melissa's suggestions as though the situation were hopeless. He had four children and the youngest ones were one and three years old. "I guess I am just stuck," he said. He then continued and told Melissa how much he admired her and wished his wife was more like she was. The compliments showered her with admiration. He then kissed her.

Melissa pushed him away and told him she did not think this was right, but the stop sign did not last long. He returned again the following week with flowers and candy, only this time the visit was for an apology for being such a "jerk," as he called himself. Melissa was touched that he thought that much of her to make the effort. She invited him in and they talked for a long time. He then hugged her, and then the kiss happened.

The affair had begun. For the first year, Bill was obsessed with Melissa and she him. He called her whenever he could and made steady dates with her once a week. He traveled far distances to be with her. He drove two hours to check into a hotel for a conference and then drove back two hours to spend the night with her. He gave her special cards, gifts and was very attentive to her. They were connected on every level that the "soul" connection allowed.

Melissa, however, saw so many strange things that caused tumultuous friction between them. His cell phone would ring, and he would glance at it and put it down. Why didn't he answer the phone in her presence? His wife called several times a day, demanding to know when he was coming home. If Bill did not call his wife at lunch, she would ask him if he forgot he had a wife. Melissa once overheard his wife telling him that she missed him.

Melissa also noticed a pattern of distance towards her. She wondered why he would not call her on Monday mornings and why he would see her one week, but the next week he generated excuses for why he could not see her. She noticed that Saturday nights she would not receive emails from him. It was not until Sunday evening that a message arrived. She thought it strange that Bill had barbeques with his wife's family on the weekends. She thought it strange that Bill's wife was constantly concerned for the children. The information came in bits and pieces and did not add up to the way Bill portrayed his home. There was a contradiction between his actions and his rhetoric. She approached Bill with her concerns and terminated the affair many times. She told him that she thought he was a liar.

Each time she ended it with him, however, she felt like she

lost a piece of herself and was overcome with sadness and grief. Bill felt the same way and would return to her with apologies. He claimed his life was just not the same without her and that he could not go on without her in his life. He said he loved her deeply and that someday they would be together.

This was an eight-year prison sentence for Melissa.

Each year the affair became worse for Melissa because Bill grew more passive in his interest in her and gave her less and less. She began to feel he had other women because his schedule became more erratic, and his moods began to shift back and forth as he went from being critical of her to admiring her. It was as though he were two people with schizophrenic emotions.

Eventually, Bill changed his schedule with Melissa. He stopped calling her all together in the mornings and on weekends. He put her on a tight schedule that only tied into his work timetable. Calls only came when he was on his way home. He then began ending it with Melissa saying that she deserved better. He would say that his wife was the mother of his children, and he could not just up and leave her after she invested so many years in him.

After all this time she invested, Bill hardly noticed her and seemed to look right through her. His desire for her grew dim as he had a planned exit right after their love making sessions. He began seeing her less, as his job and parenting pressures became stronger.

One time on a trip together Bill left Melissa and told her that he only said terrible things about his wife because he wanted to have a relationship with her. Melissa was crushed. She felt used and had.

Bill returned again a month later, promising things would change and that he was, again, not the same without her in his life. He kept his promises for two weeks and then his behaviors became worse than ever before.

This situation nearly destroyed Melissa. It destroyed her career because she was so emotionally empty, torn and depleted that she could barely focus. It destroyed her self worth because she was so broken down by his treatment that she had come to believe that (subconsciously) she was not worthy of a man's love.

Melissa lost so much. She lost her child baring years. She lost her friends because her life was taken over by Bill and his emotional toying and flip-flopping. Her career suffered. This affair turned into an addiction that was eating Melissa like a cancer. There was no escape. She was on a fast moving roller coast that continued to go up and down, and she felt like she was spinning out of control. It was as though she was not complete without Bill, but when she was with him, however, she felt rushed, like an object to please Bill. She was no longer that special woman that Bill loved more than anyone, but rather a convenience to Bill after he took care of everyone and everything else in his life.

When Melissa finally hit rock bottom, she could no longer deny how damaged she was because of her affair with Bill. She ended it and spent years trying to pick herself up from the ashes. She realized how she had been used, probably like many others before her.

This affair is a lot like a fireman in a *backdraft* situation. When the fire is burning all around him, he stands in the (deceptive) clear point fighting the fire. He can't see the danger. He thinks he has the fire contained, but low and behold there is combustion smoldering and, with a little oxygen, the fury ignites to his disadvantage. It blows up in his face. It takes skill and experience to extinguish the flames in this situation and, in some cases, it takes all the fireman has to stay alive.

The married player, like Bill, can be (metaphorically) a *backdraft* starter. His head games will eventually light Melissa aflame. Many women are naive and get burned in the explosive combustion. Melissa's story, unfortunately, is not uncommon. So many women become seduced by players that use them and toss them to the side. The worst scenario is when the naïve woman does not know she is being tossed aside.

I cannot stress enough how naïve we can become. One common fantasy women believe is that these married men love them so much, more than any other, and that they do not have sex with their wives. The truth is that most, nearly all, are having sex with their wives while they are bullshitting naïve women into keeping true to them. In some cases married players really are having celibacy in the home, but it is very rare. There is one way that you can know for sure.

If you are a woman who has gotten tangled into a mess with a married man like Melissa, all you have to do to get the truth is look at his wife's behaviors. If his wife is calling him all day, demanding answers and attention from him, then he is having a sexual and emotional relationship with her. This woman obviously wants her husband and is desperately demanding his attention. If he is not touching her and being intimate with her, she is going to fight tooth and nail for it. If he has not left her and is living in the house with her, he is going to give into her. If he didn't, there would be no peace. He would be forced to shit or get off the pot.

In Melissa's case, you can clearly see that Bill loves his wife. Much like a *cad*, he has his fun with Melissa and then switches back to the attention on his wife. This is why Melissa did not hear from Bill on the weekends or on Mondays until after he got back into the swing of work. He was in the afterglow of the weekend with his wife and kids. Melissa could be considered what some might call *work wives*. These are woman with whom men have intimate interactions at work or during his work schedule. She is in the *work pillar*.

It is also evident that Bill compartmentalized Melissa in his pillar because he had her on a calling schedule, which left his life open to take care of other things. He obviously was not committed to Melissa. It is also transparent that Bill was having an intimate relationship with his wife by the bonding of the families and the activities that were planned. A woman that does not want her husband or who has been rejected by her husband, may not routinely plan outings with other family members. Most likely she will try to avoid them in the effort to hide her marital discord.

If you put all the pieces together, you have a portrait of truth no matter what he tells you. Bill may not have been madly in love with his wife, but he did love her and was giving her something that she was craving. He lacked the balls to tell her the truth.

Most importantly, Bill may have been in love with Melissa and at the same time using Melissa to make his marriage better, which is something that can cause a mistress to do unthinkable acts. It is cruel. This is why Bill constantly told her that his life was not the same without her in it. What he was really saying was that he felt empty inside with his wife and kids and being with Melissa gave him drive and vigor to be a better husband and father. It is the fantasy escape in the mind. I have seen this happen. It is exceptionally cruel to the mistress who spends her life alone. It is cruel to the wife because he is "dreaming" of another women while pretending in the marriage with his wife.

Too often women fall for the players' lines. If more women would refuse advances from married men, then players would have fewer toys with which to play. They would be forced to confront their own misery in themselves and in their marriages. Think about this for a moment. If you are a mistress, is it enough for you to be used so that he can be a better husband to another woman? Aren't you worth more?

You must make choices that are in your own best interest. I know a woman who was very smart because she did not buy into the line that he was "saving himself for her" or that he was just there for the "sake of the kids." She refused to perform oral sex on him because she did not want her mouth down there after it had been "elsewhere," as she claimed. It did not matter, though, because he turned right around and got a blow job from his wife. Is this an honorable man? You be the judge.

Married players seduce women by telling them how bad their wives are in the hope that these women will think they could be better than their wives. It makes women feel special, needed and useful, like most need to feel. This is the bate they use. If they say they are staying for the sake of the kids, women would understand how difficult divorce is on kids and how costly it is for them. These men also know that women want to be the only ones who are loved and adored by men; therefore, they tell them that they are not having sex at all with their wives. This opens up the door for the unsuspecting woman to feel chosen and special.

Most importantly and, I will be as crude here as I was with him a while back, men love to get laid, and they love pussy. On a late Saturday night, her pussy looks as good as yours. Yours looks as good as hers. It does not matter. Many women think he is home on a late Saturday night dreaming of her, when he is enjoying his wife's pussy. I am using his crude language.

Let us take this one step further. Some women think these men are trapped at home when they really are on the internet porno sites, masturbating in the middle of the night. You can detect this if he reads your email in the middle of the night but does not respond for an hour or so. What is he doing online in the wee hours of the morning? He probably is not reading scriptures from the bible. In addition, some players have internet love affairs as well, which can be worse than sexual relationships because they are emotional connections.

Married (serial) players have all kinds of games that they play. They do some far out things that would prompt you to pause and shake your head. Sometimes it is easy for them to dangle several women on a string because they use their wives as an escape route to abandon certain girlfriends when need be.

Here a few pointers that will definitely tell you if he is having sex somewhere else: If his dick is sticky, he has been putting it someplace else. If he can last a long time before he ejaculates and has not seen you in a month, he shot off somewhere. If he hardly has any seaman when he ejaculates and has not seen you in a month, where did it all go? Who got it all? You never really know what truth is lurking when you have a married man who is screwing around on his wife and, perhaps, you too.

When something looks suspicious, there is something wrong. You must accept what you see and force yourself not to plow into denial. Look for specific things that speak to you: If he will not answer his phone in your presence, there is a real problem. Something is going on. Further, if he is unavailable on the weekends or in the mornings and has you on a tightly controlled schedule, something is going on. Be cautious. Also, if he will (routinely) not answer his phone when you call, what is the reason? Is there another woman or does he hold you in such little regard that he figures you can just wait until he feels like returning your call? This is a situation where he has total control. It is very demeaning. You must decide if this is the type of situation that brings you peace, love and joy.

If you are a mistress in this situation, the best thing you can do for yourself is get out of it as quickly as possible and don't look back. If he is not making a commitment to you, then he is not serious about you. He will eventually abandon you when he boots you out of his life. If he is putting you on a schedule, you have to ask yourself if you want to be an object that is fit into this calendar for his needs when he wants. What about your needs? If he is a married man who is playing around with you, he may be playing around with others because you know for a fact he is playing around on another woman: his wife. Most importantly, he is showing you he is not a man of honor, courage and commitment. He is nothing like the King, but rather the dysfunctional Prince. The choice is yours to make.

Mistress and Wife No More

Fair Prince, I say goodbye to you

15

Enough Defined

If you are a mistress or a wife who is emotionally attached to a player, you probably live in a world of loneliness, isolation and panic. If I were a betting woman, I would wager that your life is anything but stable and happy. You may have spurts of happiness that lead you on. You may live in a fantasy that the good times will automatically become permanent. Then, a few days later when you notice he has changed back again to a stranger, you come crashing to the ground once again. It hurts and, as I have repeated throughout this book, it can destroy your life. The truth is that being with a man who is screwing around on you or using you for his own interest makes it difficult for you in all areas of your life. The sad point I must note is that many women live in this hell subconsciously. They have no idea just how badly their men have damaged them until they have lost enough to wake up.

Once women come to the cross roads, they have the new problem of deciding what to do next. They must decide how to remove themselves from this hellish prison. Timing is everything because years come and go so quickly. It is wise if a woman gets out before she loses too much, but many women hang on until the bitter end, until there is nothing left.

Once a woman has had enough, she comes to a *done point*, as I call it. It is an invisible ending that just happens one day but, unfortunately, women have lost a lot by this point. You know you have reached this point when you are no longer angry, hurt or sad. When you look at him with pity, you have reached acceptance. The truth, (when it comes strong enough that you finally let it in), will set you free. You will then let him go. Your decision will be made as quickly as you watched him changed many times right before your eyes, and it is then, surprisingly enough, that your problems will begin.

When he senses he is losing you (for good this time), he will panic and pursue you with promises like never before. Remember: He may not want you or anyone else to abandon him. If you have finally reached the done point, there will be no return for him. This is the point when some women have battled harassment and stalking behaviors. It is at this stage that you may have a difficult time getting him out of your life.

Dangling Chains

The purpose of this book is to help women recognize the metal chains dangling so that they can escape now before losing everything. The first step is to take personal inventory. Are you involved with a married player or a married wimp? Are you involved with a religious man that will never make the break from his wife? Perhaps you are the wife who knows her husband is running around.

No matter what the circumstances surrounding your life, you need to determine if you are happy. Let us explore this further. Are you getting what you want from your relationship? Are you fulfilled? Do you feel loved, respected and cherished by the man to whom you are committed? A wise person once told me you can never go wrong if you answer (in advance) the following four questions:

1. What is it that I want?

2. How do I get it in an honest, transparent manner?

3. Am I willing to put forth the effort and do what it takes to get it?

4. Will I be happy once I get it?

I will add one more: Am I willing to walk away if I am not getting what I want? It is only when you rid your closet of dirt that you can make room for the "clean." If you are still holding on to old wounds from your childhood, you will attract more painful relationships into your life. If you do not analyze the relationships you had with the father figure in your life, you will attract more *bad boy* men to pose as the charming Prince. And we know how this ends.

You must first take inventory and look at your needs.

Become your own woman with dreams, hopes, and interests and then seek a compatible mate. If you want the married man you are now with, then smoke him out. Be strong and patient. Most importantly, be willing to *not* get what you want in the long run. A man either wants you or he doesn't. If he wants you but is unwilling to commit to you, then he does not want you enough. This is no reflection on you as a person because he may be so wrapped in his own world of fear that he cannot break free. It may also be a reflection of the two of you together: It may be too late. As my mother always said: When one door closes, another opens.

Dost Thou Love me?

True love somehow always finds a way to surface on top. It is important women understand that unconditional love is a way of life, not just a roll in the hay and phone calls every now and then. It cannot be compartmentalized in a pillar because it is continual energy that takes no form. Therefore, it cannot be contained or measured. What does this mean to you?

First, if a man is in love with you, he radiates when you are near him. He can't keep himself away from you. He is drawn to you in a room, much like a moth gravitates to the flame.

If a man loves you, he defends your honor and puts you before others. He takes interest in you and makes your needs a priority. When you need him, he drops everything to be there for you. He plans a life with you, not just a dinner date and a scheduled three hours in bed with you.

If he loves you, he touches you more often, and not just where the sun does not shine. It is less of a sexual love and more of an intimate love. If he loves you, he puts your sexual pleasure before his own and, after the loving, he nudges your body closer to his. He can't get enough of you. As the song by Engelbert Humerdinck preaches: *After the lovin,' I'm still in love with you.*

If a man truly loves you, he feels your presence when you are gone. Ronald Ragan used to claim that he felt lonely every time Nancy walked out of the room. This is true love. It is a partnership, a companion, a best friend, and the other half of you. If he truly loves you, he feels a part of him is missing when he is not with you.

If a man loves you, he remembers the little things about you and talks fondly of you to others. He plans events where he will bring you to meet his friends and family. Given that a man strives to please his woman, he will do whatever to please the woman he truly loves. Most importantly, he will always return to the woman he loves, much like a lost horse in the wild that keeps finding his way home.

If a man truly loves you, then you are the first one he wants to see in the morning and last one he wants to talk to at night. He has serious intentions with you and does not let anyone or anything stand in between your relationship, not even his kids

(And you should not come between him and his kids, either).

I think the best indicator of true love comes from within you. You know when a man loves you, just like you know in your gut when a man doesn't love you. If he loves you, you feel it. If you are going with a married man, you know if he loves you.

When discussing a man and true love in the same sentence, I can't leave out the abstract noun *fear*. It is important to note, though, that love and fear cannot exist in the same space. If he is so afraid of his wife's reaction or is so consumed with guilt for "leaving" his kids, he will end up the miserable one. He will remain stuck in the space of fear, forever longing for the love with you. This is unfortunate. I have known many adults who, when reflecting on their childhood years, claim they wish their parents would have divorced because now they are spending years in therapy trying to "undo" the damage of *staying together for the sake of the kids*.

With all this being said, only you can decide what is right for you. You have to decide if you want to hang on to a man that feels guilty for loving you. Do you want to waste your years?

If you are a wife, you know in your soul if your husband is truly in love with you or if he is stuck on another woman. You deserve more than to be an ornament in the house that caters to his every whim. If you have sensed for a period of time that he is in love with another woman, do you need him to come forward to confess?

Only you can be the judge of your situation. The best thing you can do is take inventory of your life and decide what changes you need to make. Plan ahead and take action for yourself.

Faithful
Relationships

"Only until death do we part", said the faithful
King

16

Digging Up Our Past

The best way to plan a better future is to study the past. This is true in any setting, no matter what the topic. If we understand the past and study what worked and what did not work, we can better arm ourselves with the tools to make wiser choices. If we study relationships and what has worked for couples, we can apply this information to ourselves. Let us return to history.

When I was a freshman in college completing my undergraduate work, I took a boring course (so I thought at the time) called *Digging Up Our Past*, a course in anthropology, which studied our ancestors from cave times. I did not have enough life experience to appreciate what the course had to offer back then, but I can appreciate it now. This class examined the sociological and psychological factors of our homosapian ancestors through archaeological findings. The artifacts that were found in caves and remote areas of the world paint a vivid picture of how our ancestors cohabitated. The information from the class, along with with a summarization of Dr. John Gray's philosophy and theories (*Men are from Mars and Women are from Venus*), should be applied to our discussion about men and women.

In cave men days, for example, men and women had three functions: eat, sleep and reproduce. The primary function of the man was to spend endless time each day hunting for food. His primary job was to hunt for food. After his hard day's labor, he came home to a woman who appreciated his effort for putting his life on the line.

The woman's duty, on the other hand, was to make a comfortable hut or village by gathering the necessities for shelter. After she spent the day cooking and making a "cozy" home, she felt adored by her man.

Together, they reproduced. It worked like a gem because here we are a million years later. What has changed?

Much to our surprise, nothing has changed. It is sad, however, that men and women have forgotten the secrets that kept our ancestors together. We have evolved to such a degree that we now neglect our primary needs. As a result, the divorce rate has quadrupled and the infidelity rate has skyrocketed. If you want to study more on this topic, Dr. John Gray's books *Mars and Venus* discuss this theory at length. It has been years since I read his books, but I still remember the brilliance in this man's philosophy. His books are shockingly accurate and a most entertaining read.

In today's society, women no longer depend on men to sit on a rock in the woods all day (facing great danger) to kill a buffalo for food. We go to Stater Brothers, Shop Rite, Winn Dixie or Vons for that big steak. Further, men no longer depend on women to sit at home all day cooking and sewing because we have Macy's and various department stores to supply our clothing needs. Truth be told, we do not need one another like they did in the cave. We have subconsciously lost touch with our need for each other; yet, we still have the same basic needs as men and women.

To further capitulate, when men and women both venture out to work each day, they find support from coworkers, clients, and others. We no longer depend primarily on one another for protection, comfort and support. This puts a strain on relationships because outside parties become the *keepers of our feelings*, should we need to "get things off of our chest." Further, career opportunities in this era are endless, which allows couples to stray in different career directions. Therefore, it may become more difficult for couples to relate to one another on a professional level. When the stress mounts each day, our partner may not have the professional insight to provide the support for which we long. It may become more comfortable to confide in coworkers because they are better able to relate to our professional settings. When we return to our spouses in the evenings, we may have already debriefed our emotional stress with someone else, or we may need to debrief and unload to someone who understands the situation.

If the emotional support is not there, women may feel neglected and men may feel deprived; thus, they may both withhold from one another. Men have the tendency to withdraw and crave more space. Women, on the other hand, may feel threatened by this distance and withhold sex because they feel neglected. If small disputes go unchecked, the rift grows larger. Before we know it, men are looking at the beauty in other women, and women are seeking emotional support from other men. The bottom line is that communication, emotional connection, is the cord that connects us.

No matter how we look at it, men still need to feel appreciated, needed and glamorized for their efforts, and women still need to feel protected, appreciated and adored. In this fast paced society, we lose sight of this.

I would also like to note that, despite women's liberation efforts, men and women are not equal. This is not a sexist remark, but rather a factual statement that capitulates on hormonal and physiological differences. Men are physically stronger because they have more muscle mass and less fat. Women have more fat and less agility due to child rearing. On a deeper level, women guide relationships because they are more emotional and nurturing than men. Think about the first relationship a man has ever had. It was with his mother. He remembers this at a subconscious level and will forever seek the comfort of the womb. You are the womb.

Dear Universe

With all this talk about staying away from the bad boys, where on earth do you find the good ones? This is the most difficult answer because every "happily" married couple has a unique answer. Some people meet through friends; many people meet through work; a lot of singles meet at church or religious functions. Some people meet at weddings, barmitzvahs, or other celebration get-togethers. Some meet in college or extracurricular classes. Some meet at Wal Mart, Home Depot, or other stores. Many meet at online dating web sites. Some of the online dating sites are very helpful because honorable men will not pay good money and spend two hours filling out personal profiles if they just want to "get laid," as I once heard a player tell his buddy. Some people, as desperate as it may sound, write letters to the universe asking love to find them. Anything that works, go for it!

Before you go on your first date, you may want to decide if he is worth it. For example, if a man has been married five times, a wise woman knows that there may be a seventh, as she may be the unlucky sixth. You have to decide if it is worth your time. You may also want to evaluate his history of love relationships. If he is still single in his fifties, this may be a red flag. Is he afraid of commitment? Is he gay or bisexual? Is he married to bottles of booze? If no woman ever managed to "settle" him, then what is his first love? Is he still living at home with his mother at forty-six years old? If so, this may be a bright red flag that something is wrong. You may want to decide if he is worth your time, effort and, perhaps, risk. If he is a real charmer with a shady past, you may run the risk of getting sucked into another "player" situation. Protect yourself. You may want to avoid situations that have red flags right from the start.

A wise woman knows what she wants beforehand. If you don't want a drunk, then don't go to bars to meet men. You must know what habits you can tolerate and those that you can't. For example, if you can't stand cigarette smoke and your "man of interest" is smoking a cigarette, then you must decide if you can tolerate the smoke. If you know he smokes and proceed to get involved with him anyway, then you are agreeing to his habit. If you think you can get him to quit, you will have problems. The reality is that the man smokes cigarettes. If you can't tolerate the smoke, then move on to a nonsmoker. Once we seek to change someone, we take a sledge hammer to the relationship. Know your limitations and what you can tolerate.

If you need to buy an outfit for an occasion, you must know the event ahead of time so you can buy "appropriately." If you want a "good" relationship, then you need to know ahead of time what type of man you want. Just as we suggested to the men earlier, make a list of the qualities you want in a mate. What kind of man will "complete" you? Most importantly, you may want to take out your inventory list that you completed earlier and seek opposite traits of those *bad boy* men who have broken your heart so many times before. If you find yourself bored and uncomfortable with your date, this may be a positive sign. The more "bored" you feel, the more you may want to pursue him. He may be a good guy who does not have the dysfunctional skills to put you on a roller coaster ride. If, on the other hand, you feel comfortable with him, like you are right at home, you may end up in the same situation all over again. It is the old familiar territory. And we know how this ends.

When you really set your mind to finding a good mate and you are ready for love, I believe it will find you. Try all avenues. Employ patience while avoiding desperation. Remember, you are your own first love.

Once you find Mr. Right, you have to make sure he is not Mr. Wrong. Many women that came from dysfunctional backgrounds lack "interviewing skills" during the dating phase. This is when you weed out the good from the bad and the weak from the strong. This is when you walk forward or run like hell the other way. Let us discuss this. My friend recently dated a man who, within the first half hour of their meeting, had one margarita and two beers. If a man can drink this much in thirty minutes, how much is he going to drink in two hours? This was a red flag. Again, if you don't want a drunk, then watch how much he drinks during dinner. This will give you the answer.

Once you meet a man you find interesting, watch everything you can. When you are on your first date, watch how he orders his food. Is he polite and respectful? Is he controlling and analytical of every single move you make? Does he tell you how to order or comment on how you did not do something correctly? If so, you may want to end the date right then and there. Is he rude and offensive? Does he flirt with the waitress? Does he watch other women come and go in the restaurant? These questions will tell you much about him.

Notice his relationship to technical devices that connect him to other people. Does he have his cell phone on and what does he do when it rings? Does he have an elaborate cell phone with expensive gadgets for texting and mobile email and all other modes of communication? One thing that was a "positive" with the *Mr. Drinker* date was that he had an older cell phone without added features and, I might add, he had no idea how to text. This suggests he was not a player who had several women dangling at the other end of this phone. If a man's phone is constantly ringing and he is not on call for his job, then the red flag is waving in your face. If something does not feel right, then it is not right. Trust your instincts.

You may also listen carefully to what he says. Is he

constantly admiring you and filling you with compliments? Is he charming and charismatic, or is he down-to-earth and interested in what you have to say? The last thing you need is another charmer who *bullshits* his way into your life with phoniness. You may want to make sure he has the direct opposite traits of the player you were with.

Analyze his personality traits. Is he fickle and indecisive? How does he handle situations? An honorable man usually knows what he wants and takes action to get it. If he does not know, he won't pretend he does. He will, however, take action to find out. I once knew a Prince Charmer who wooed all the ladies and, once he felt comfortable enough with them, he would tell them he had been badly hurt and did not know if he wanted a serious relationship at the time. He set these women up. He should have removed himself from the playing field before the first inning. If he tells you that he has been hurt and really does not want a committed relationship now, he is telling you he just wants to get laid, pardon the straight-forward diction. Run like hell.

Listen to what he has to say. What type of conversations does he initiate? Does he jump from one thing to another without listening to anything you say? Is he interested in you, or is he interested in how you look? There is a huge difference. If you watch his eyes and where his vision pulls him, you will have your answer. Is he consistent with his stories, or does he say one thing and then thirty minutes later contradict his previous statements? You do not need another liar. Run like hell. Does he constantly boost about himself and his achievements? This is not a good sign. You do not need a narcissist.

You may also want to evaluate your own demeanor. For example, if you wear a low cut blouse that shows your breasts and skin tight pants that outline the female anatomy between your legs, what are you saying to him? If you package yourself with respect and dignity, then he will treat you as such. If he still looks for places the sun does not shine, he is telling you what he is after. The choice is yours to make.

You may also want to explore his close relationships. What does he say about his mother and father? Is he complimentary of them and of his upbringing? This may give you insight to his experiences. To be fair, many men have had painful pasts but have worked through tough spots. The key is know if they have cleaned out the baggage to make room for the "clean."

It is a good idea to explore his relationship with money, too. How does he handle his money? Does he say that he is in debt beyond his control and is trying to get his finances in order? The way he handles his money may be indicative of the way he handles the rest of his life. Further, does he work? How many jobs has he had and for how long? This may provide some insight as to how stable and responsible he is?

A good way to weed out the bad is to watch how he handles his anger. How does he react if he was overcharged for something? This gives you an indication of how he treats others. Everyone gets angry, but it is how we cope with our anger that tells who we are. If he shows any sign of having an explosive temper, this is probably a warning sign. The last thing many women want is a temperamental, nasty, angry man that is always looking for an argument. If, on the other hand, he tells you that he never gets angry, you may really have a red flag. Anger is a natural emotion and anyone who does not have it, may not be able to feel it. This, in turn, could signify passive aggressive behavior. If you have just been squashed by a player, you may know this all too well.

Think about your conversation. Is it positive, or are you talking about all the "wrong" in the world that he would like fix? If so, he may be a negative person. How he behaves now is very important. You want a positive, productive man who will enhance your life. A wise woman will leave the angry ones (who want to fight the world) right where she found them.

Evaluate his "packaging." How does his appearance look? Is he preoccupied with image? Players have a tendency to be preoccupied with looks; they can be very critical. It is time you found a good, honorable, down-to-earth guy who will accept you.

The most important thing I must ask is: Are you

compatible? Do you have the same interests, passions, goals, and desires? If he tells you he came from a dysfunctional home and never wants to have kids, listen to him. If you want three or four children, this is not the guy for you. If you think you can "comfort" him from his painful childhood and make him love you enough to change his mind about children, you may be setting yourself up for pain. Keep in mind, as we said earlier, women have a tendency to manipulate people. As we can see from this book, look at where this gets most women. It is now time to grab what is right for you and discard that which is not.

Examine his personal qualities. Is he genuine, real and honest, or does he tell you what you want to hear? If you listen long enough to him, you will have the answers. Further, is there chemistry between you? Do you feel comfortable? If things went well, you may want to make plans for a second date. Within the next few weeks, you may want to test him in various areas. If you can get a hold of him on the weekends, this will tell you that he is single and unattached. If you visit his home and explore his personal space, this will paint a picture of who he is. If you call his work and ask for him, this will tell you if he really works where he says he does. Remember, if you are dating a stranger, you will need to check him out, much like a prospective employer checks references on an employee of interest.

A wise woman makes sure his story adds up before she

invests any further in him. She may also want to meet his friends and family to see what they say about him. The best way to get to know a man is to watch him interact in different personal settings with those closest to him.

Remember that it is not how he perceives you, but how you perceive him that should determine if there is a second date.

Until Death Do We Part

If we desire faithful relationships, we must choose wisely and understand our basic needs as men and women. No matter where we go, our instinctive needs are still the same as they were a million years ago. I do not know of a woman anywhere that does not want to be held, protected, loved, wanted and adored by a man. And every man I have ever met has the desire to be appreciated by his woman. He needs her to validate him as a man and confirm that he is meeting her needs. He also needs his space to love her without being smothered and forced to return to her.

Faithful relationships thrive on compatibility, respect, understanding, support, acceptance, nurturing and space. If our partner is also our best friend, then we have it made. The commitment is strong; the desire to run home is overwhelming. Men will have little desire to stray, and women will have every desire to nest where they are.

If you want a faithful relationship, choose a faithful mate and nurture each other. As I said earlier in this book, not all

men are unfaithful. There are reasons men are unfaithful.
Maybe he is an otherwise honorable man or maybe he is just a
player, but most men desire faithful relationships where they
can feel safe, loved, appreciated and affirmed. Even the hard-
core players long for this, and this is why they bounce all over
the place. If you understand this, then you will be the keeper of
his heart. Whether it is your married lover, husband, or another
single man you meet someday, he will still have the same
instinctive needs of every other man.

Most women I have known simply do not understand the
male species. I would like to share my secret with you based on
my experiences with men. Men are a lot like horses. They may
stand stubbornly by themselves and refuse to budge at times.
They don't want to be bothered, coaxed, moved, manipulated or
anything else that brings them out of themselves if they are in a
"focused" mood. If we invade their space, they will move away
or run. If we pull at them, they will become agitated and may
buck. If we leave them alone and do not move toward them,
they will eventually move closer to us. They cannot stand the
fact that we are standing still, even though they need to be alone
at times. If you do not believe me, test it. If he does not call you,
do not call him. Wait. See how long it takes for him to come
back to you if you do not run to him asking that loaded
question, *"Why didn't you call?"* If he comes home from work
and goes right into his den, leave him there. Do not barge in

and say "Honey, how was your day? How come you didn't greet me? Why didn't you kiss me hello? What is the matter? Why didn't you call me today at lunch?" See how long it takes him to come into the other room where you are. It will not be long. When he has collected himself, he will look around to see where you are. Horses always return. When you do not ask questions, he will give answers. He will love you more for allowing him the freedom to be who he is without being smothered by you for constant reassurance.

You do not need reassurance if you have a man that feels you meet his needs. He will, in turn, meet your needs and the relationship will prosper and will be able to withstand the peeks and valleys of the *Until Death Do We Part* oath that you took at the alter or the one you wish to take in the future.

www.ingramcontent.com/pod-product-compliance
Lightning Source LLC
Chambersburg PA
CBHW060736050426
42449CB00008B/1251